Playwork Inspired Learning

Chris Watkins

Playwork Inspired Learning
ISBN: 978-1-8381658-0-2

First published in Great Britain
in 2020 through Amazon
self-publishing service

Disclaimer: real names/places
have been changed to protect the identities.

Produced by samanthahoughton.co.uk

Dedications

I would like to dedicate this to Lucy Beth Dale, the best second mum to my children and her beautiful little lady, to my children's dad, Wayne, for meeting such an amazing lady (and for being an amazing dad!).

Ang and Gerald Packer for always being the best ever family I could ever meet and for loving me for who I am.

Caren, we are achieving so much more than we ever realised just by being ourselves - who'd have thought it!?

Steph, you are an amazing lady; strong, courageous and going through an incredible transformation too - *"we got this."*

To my friend from what feels like a lifetime ago, Sarah Lawrence, you really are the truest lifelong friend I have ever had, you are like a sister to me.

My children, Faith, Katy and Mikey, you will never know how incredible you all are.

Contents

Acknowledgements

I would like to thank every lecturer that I have ever worked with. Despite you never knowing that this is where my studies would take me, I am grateful for the time you gave to me, the inspiration, and the opportunity to keep pushing myself forward. I would like to thank every professional I have spoken to about my approach and the encouragement to finally pull it all together to write a book.

This book has been a long time coming, many years in fact! I would never have been able to do it if it wasn't for my *'three amigos'* Karen Harris, Carrie Mayo and Amy Medd, because they helped me to come up with Playwork Inspired Learning's title and cover. If it were not for you, I would never have come up with something quite as fantastic as we did as a team. I dearly love you all and between us, we have made something incredible. Also, thanks to my team members past and present for taking the time to learn this approach.

Yes, I know that it was I that wrote it, but you are a large part of this too.

I would like to say a huge thankyou to Sam Houghton, not only in helping me with the fine details of this book but also becoming a lovely friend and supporter. You have inspired me, encouraged me and given me the confidence to really say *'I know this!'* Also to Debs Bamford for introducing us right at the beginning of this project and also for being a fantastic friend and supporter in our many calls and chats over the years.

My support team, you have always been there and always have my back. You will never know just how lucky I am to have you at my side.

I would also like to thank my nan (Ann Crimble) and my late grandad (Norman Crimble), you gave me the most incredible opportunities to just play. I know that you don't think you did, but you both made a huge difference in my life.

Foreword

To say that I'm delighted to have been asked to write this forward is an understatement. I feel truly honoured, not only because Chris is a friend, but also because we share a deep passion in the value of play for all children. I believe that practitioners of every stage or level in their career can enrich and strengthen their understanding of the importance of play presented in this book.

For me, I came to enter into the world of Childcare by first volunteering at my daughter's pre-school. Later I obtained a Level 3 Certificate in Childcare whilst working part-time at Frittenden Pre-School (in Kent) and part-time at an engineering company. However, I knew that being a Childcare Practitioner was my true ambition. I left the engineering industry to pursue my career in Childcare and was offered a permanent position at Frittenden Pre-school. Whilst loving my time there and being involved in the education and play of children, I was not innately enamoured with the *'tick the box'* system of the *Early Years Foundation Stage (DfE 2017)*

Why couldn't the children just have uninterrupted play?

Why did they have to be in a certain age bracket to accomplish a task?

Did this mean that I wasn't able to *'tick'* them off because they were considered too young?

Why were children not permitted to learn at their own pace?

Having the adults set up 2-3 activities before the children were there did not make a lot of sense when most children under 5 have differing interests. I began to find that I needed answers to these questions. As my family grew, I chose to become an Ofsted Registered Childminder and Petite Stars Childminding in Lamberhurst was born. My approach to learning became very much child-led play with myself in the background observing the children engaged in each task. Unbeknown to me, this practice had been around for some time. I was first introduced to Playwork whilst attending an

Out of School Course. A gentleman by the name of Stuart Lester, a Senior Lecturer in Play and Playwork, who later became my tutor, introduced me to the idea that play should be just that – play. Play is often utilised within the education system and is structured by adults with specific outcomes, as we see in the *EYFS (DfE 2017)*. As *Stuart Lester writes in Play for a Change 2008 'play in its most raw form promotes healthy physical, social, emotional and cognitive development naturally'.*

Stuart ended his speech by promoting a Masters Degree in Playwork. I entered, and this is how I met Chris. She has become not only a life-long friend but one who has gone on to achieve her Masters in Playwork. I could not be more proud and incredibly pleased for her. Chris is an exceptional advocate in the importance of play for children, which shows in her written works. This wonderful woman has not only built up her own nursery from scratch whilst raising her own children, she has also continued to grow her knowledge in Playwork by exploring theories, discussing, and researching this useful tool we can now all share.

Through Chris' book, I hope and believe that many discussions and questions will be had amongst practitioners all over the country. This, in turn, will lead to discussions inside Ofsted and the DfE about the use of play within the *EYFS (DfE 2017)*.

Chris takes us inside her theory of Playwork, introducing it properly and explains how Playwork can be developed for the benefit of younger children. Here she explores with real-life examples and thoughtful analysis on how Playwork is not only beneficial for those children age 5-12 years but also how you can use Playwork to best suit those we care for under the age of 5. We get a great understanding of each phase of her work and her theories surrounding the use of Playwork. There are questions that let practitioners reflect on children's play in their own settings and environments, and how we as adults interpret play. It also enables us to achieve a broader understanding of how Play and Playwork, although different actually work along-side each other. Chris invites us into her Nursery where the implementation of Playwork is used and shows us that some ideas have not worked whereas others have flourished.

Chris has produced a powerful tool for scenarios and sustained practitioner development. She has focused on a core belief that should belong in the repertoire of all practitioners. After all *'We are the managers of the world's greatest resource: Children' (Robert John Meehan).* I believe this book can help practitioners develop a shared vision and understanding of how playwork can compliment play and in turn, promote discussions on its use in under 5's.

Chris has written this book and is true to herself. It's as if we were having a conversation face to face. The structure of her writing, her examples and how flexible the use of Playwork can be, lend this book to be used as a guide for practitioners, to question, discuss, observe and analyse their practices.

In short, Chris' book offers a different approach to play in its most raw forms. And what a better way for practitioners to strengthen their knowledge and understanding than learning just how important and how magical play is to our children. My hope is that this book will become a lifeline in a practitioners arsenal of books. (I for one will be implementing the use of this book for my own business) and you, the reader, the practitioner, will take inspiration from this wonderful lady and use it to help you develop your skills in the art of Playwork Inspired Learning.

Amy Osborne

Ofsted registered childminder of Petite Stars Childminding

1

Why should you listen to me?

From an early age I had access to adventure playgrounds, woods, beaches and a local park which provided opportunities to play. I created play activities for my sisters to enjoy in the local community, whist still being a child myself. As a child of a parent with significant mental health issues, providing play for my sisters was my way to avoid being at home for long periods of time, therefore, the more creative the opportunity, the longer my siblings were kept occupied and out of trouble for being noisy at home. However, my grandparents provided rich opportunities - not only for my siblings, but it gave me the chance to also be playful. They both gave us all the necessary space and time to develop our own play, whether it be with cardboard, tape recorders to create our own stories or a huge garden with a boat within the parameters, so we could play pirates. These memories are a huge part of my childhood memory bank and I have used their ideas throughout my life when looking after children. These plentiful opportunities gave me and my sisters the chance to *'play out'* different situations and eventually create my own form of play therapy. I was using play to develop ways of dealing with situations that were out of my control, supporting and promoting my own well-being and resilience as I looked after and promoted the same feelings of safety for my siblings.

As the years passed, I watched children I used to babysit, create and develop their own play with me as a player, and other times as the teenager that was taking care of them. As I got older (note, not growing up), being playful in nature was normal to me. When I had my first child in 2003, I volunteered at Sure Start in the city of Southampton. Sure Start worked alongside families with children under the age of four - providing support to families who needed assistance in managing their lives while responsible for young children and to develop confidence in their ability to do so. It was also developed to enable adults and children to flourish with parental support and encouraging socialisation between other adults and children with help from *'a friendly face.'* I was part of a group of support workers within a large community that involved large scale deprivation and many different cultures; I assisted in the toy library, family support and music groups, eventually opening a stay and play session within the tower block I lived in.

In 2005, my family and I relocated to Gloucestershire, moving from an area of high deprivation to one that had almost none; however, in this case I was the stranger in the area with less support than I was accustomed to giving. I had the opportunity to become the parent I believed I should be - enabling freedom, flexibility and opportunity for my daughter, whilst remaining a stay at home parent due to being pregnant with my son.

I began the next phase of my childcare journey in 2008, the day after becoming a single parent. Myself and a friend co-minded at her house together until circumstances changed (she got pregnant, and her children changed schools), I then became a solo minder at my own house whilst looking after my own children. Shortly after, I took on a member of staff just because the job of being a solo parent and a childminder can be a lonesome journey, especially when my way of working, focused on how children use the space around them to learn, how they manipulate toys and activities to how they want to, rather than being told how to with specific ideas and intentions from adults. This is where I first got the opportunity to share with another practitioner my personal thoughts on children, and the way I believed children learned best - at their own pace and on their own unique journey. Once I had become confident in my ethos and discussed this with parents and children, my setting became popular within the community; slowly expanding from my small three bedroomed house to a five-bedroom house to accommodate one child, and then again a few months later when a number of my parents had become pregnant. With the change in circumstance it then triggered the change between a childminder, into childcare on domestic premises, going from six children a day to twenty-four each day. The practitioners and parents loved the way the setting worked and the strong ethos of children's play being the sole basis for learning. I had begun the process of recognising that this may be an under developed theory and researched thoroughly until I realised that this way of learning did not exist.

As the business was happily going from strength to strength with the fantastic team I worked with, I applied to study for a Foundation Degree in Early Childhood Studies at University, to learn more theoretical histories and developments, that I considered may be helpful to assist in further developing the setting. I did this with the hope to develop my understanding in the wider field of early years.

The course was working well alongside the business but as I approached the second year, a bombshell hit - my landlady decided she was going to sell the home I lived in; my children, my home and the business were thrown into a state of confusion. I had to move home and either close or relocate the business.

It was then a manic search for a new home and a business setting. I managed to move into a new home whilst the setting was being converted, but it was a significantly crazy time; I finished my foundation degree, applied to get on a masters' course, whilst shutting down one setting, opening a temporary location, and building another. In my personal life, I had to overcome homelessness and relocate myself and my children to find a home in the space of a couple of months.

Upon the course recommendation of a lecturer from my Foundation degree course, I enrolled on an MA Professional Studies in Children's Play and Playwork. Again, my main drive for entering this course was to develop my own ideas and the role of play within my setting, rather than focusing on play in children from 5-12, which the course was intended for.

During this huge transitional time for me personally, professionally and work wise; one thing remained consistent - play.

Throughout my entire life play has been an extraordinary feature within my life. Understanding play and learning to further develop the psychological benefits for developing resilience, well-being and confidence, ensured that I made it through my childhood, as well as my sister doing so, despite the odds. As I grew older, recognising the huge impact it made for myself and the children I had spent years looking after, I learned to recognise that I had been using Playwork from an incredibly young age. I just did not understand the theoretical perspective behind it.

Over the years, practitioners that I know, colleagues and friends that understand the way I work and the benefits of the Playwork approach I use, have told me to publish this unique way of thinking. However, I did not feel qualified enough to justify a book.

With over 20 years' experience of working with children (it didn't feel appropriate to say my childhood counts as experience, as I had no clue what I was doing, only accepting that, that was the way to protect myself and my sisters), gaining a Foundation degree and finally, a Masters as well, I feel that now the time is right.

2

A brief history of Playwork Inspired learning

This hasn't always been its name; over the years it has been known as many things such as the Watkins theory and the Monster theory of childcare (my business name). I had many conversations about the name with some of my closest friends and from these discussions we all worked together to decide what this approach should be called; collectively we came up with Playwork Inspired Learning. This was simply because there is a lot of Playwork involved; it worked perfectly with the ethos of Playwork, early play and some of my own developed ideas.

During this period, I wrote down everything that I did and the purpose behind it to develop my own approach; using my childhood to drive the benefits of this as well. However, I felt it was not enough to just believe in it myself, so I went to university as I wanted academic clout behind me to justify how significantly relevant and important it is; it was only through many years of study that I realised my way of working was not completely unique. Well, it is, and it is not! Therefore, it became an approach rather than a theory (I would love to say theory though as it would be the first new theory in many, many years). As previously mentioned, I have been in practice for more years than I have been in academic study, so if anything, I know this approach like the back of my hand and enriched it with theoretical knowledge from constant reading, researching and relating it to years of documenting what I did from practice. A lot of the research and the approach itself has been created by me, but much more belongs to other theories I have found along the way.

Playwork is notably not academic and has never been used with children under the age of five, until now. Elements of Playwork have been introduced to early years, such as loose part play (Nicholson, 1971) when children play with small objects such as nuts, bolts, wood chippings and large items such as logs, planks and crates to create their own play, and natural resources play, but they have been tweaked to fit and sometimes are not used how they were originally intended to be, such as ornate tuff tray pre-designed activities. However, I have found a way to bring theories of Playwork into early years, not only enhancing opportunities for the children, but changing the whole balance in how the setting operates. This is done by bringing calm to practitioners, passion and excitement to the children and making the relationships between the adults and children into ones that are built on deeper levels of trust and commitment. This further allows everyone to be enablers of play.

Playwork inspired learning is an approach which encompasses several theories to make one unique approach which, is solely based on a deeper psychological understanding for play and early childhood development than are currently recognised within the practice of early years.

We all know that play is important for children, it enables them to *"learn better,"* to try more, engage with their environment and establishes a child led learning approach. The age of the children we work with are not ready for schooling, but there is a way to track their development with a much more hands off approach than currently exists. The Early Years Foundation Stage *(DfE, 2017)* gives us a framework to work to, but this focuses far too much on literal development rather than holistic development, such as a child's well-being, self-confidence, resilience and how they are in their own ability. The early years' sector has focused on play for a few years, however, the government has turned this into a learning opportunity rather than for what it is. Practitioners use play for opportunities for children to achieve, but also use play to teach and develop outcomes.

It is fair to say, with many years of experience and of gaining a Playwork qualification, play should not and cannot be defined other than the work of a child. We adults have assumed it has a meaning or definition, but this is more often than not, created by our own experiences of childhood. This is not a bad thing, there have been many theorists over hundreds of years that have done the same thing; this is how theories have been developed. I am not suggesting I have created a theory (again, I don't believe I have), I have just used experience and as just discussed, a little of my childhood to help establish the importance of play for the benefit of early childhood. Theory or not, Playwork inspired learning WILL change a child's life because it is using their key developmental years to put in place the foundations which will last them their whole lives - academically, holistically and spiritually.

3

Why Playwork Inspired Learning?

Before children are born, they are learning through sounds, emotions and the foods we eat. However, children are naturally born to play and investigate their surroundings; this was researched by *K Groos in 1919*. Primarily he researched and observed animals - noting how the animal plays to learn roles within the pack i.e. rough play teaches the lion hierarchy and the thresholds of pain and tolerance, it also practices predatory games such as chase and hunting in their cub period to develop adult hunting skills. They learn all of this in order to cope as a mature lion; but this is practiced in many different parts of the animal kingdom.

Groos states *"the very existence of youth is due in part to the necessity for play; the animal does not play because he is young, he has a period of youth because he must play" (Groos, 1919).*

This is also reiterated by many other theorists, one example of this is John Dewey (1900). He believed play is a subconscious activity that helps an individual mentally and socially - but should remain separate from work, as play helps a child into the working world. Furthermore, recognising adults may not need to play, often seeking amusement from their occupation.

When researching for my dissertation, I found one document that astonished me. I had always been under the belief that Playwork had been explored within the early years and, perhaps, disregarded as too complex to try and blend the two fields. Or maybe no one had explored its rich potential and therefore research of the two was never researched fully, as I had never been able to find documentation that could either support or push Playwork out of being used in the early years. I had spent years looking, to find out for myself. However, what made me recognise the latter was true, was in the Colorado Paper *(Sturrock and Else, 1998, p16)*. The papers introduction states this:

"In our opinion, the position of Playwork in the United Kingdom is fraught. Playwork has failed to flourish for the following reasons:

- *Our inability to constitute the functions of Playwork as a widely accepted discipline*
- *Our failure to carry off any kind of successful campaign or political lobby*
- *The rise of play care as a solution to the social problem of the working parent and the resulting impact on slender resources for play*
- *The inability of the field itself to take on and advance the movement through meaningful research and development"*
  (Sturrock and Else, 1998 p2).

Whilst the paper tries to disseminate the different benefits of Playwork using different theories to develop the idea, it is my belief that this book is the foundation for quality research within the early years' sector. Since this paper was written, the prevalence of play schemes and holiday play clubs have increased - therefore the prevalence of play has become better recognised. However, it is not embedded within early years practice as yet. Most of Playwork study can be significantly academic, therefore if you want to read about it for pleasure, the subject is quite difficult to read which can be off-putting for the general reader. Even at university level, unless you are deeply interested in Playwork as an approach, it can still be misunderstood as it can be quite complex. One of my colleagues, who I had studied with believed she understood what Playwork was, yet, after reading my dissertation finally realised the true benefit of what this theory could do for early years.

I have never understood the actual difference between play and Playwork. After reading your paper I have a much clearer idea of them.

I understand that the play the adults see children doing to relax is believed not to be useful to learning (outside early years especially); Practitioners however, know that play is important and part of learning, but without understanding the dynamics of play, how it evolves and how to support it (as in don't set it up and allow them to get on with it), this is why it is not recognised as being an important framework when it should actually underpin everything!! I really agree with you...it does need to be taught to adults who work with children to better support them. *(Cocks, 2019)*

Playwork Inspired Learning is the bridge between Playwork and early years, bringing huge benefits for children under the age of five. My colleague at the time was also an early years provider whilst also studying alongside me. Another colleague I studied with was qualified in Playwork whilst working within early years and despite being already knowledgeable about Playwork (whereas I was still limited in my knowledge), raved about the benefit of Playwork. Justifiably so, she was upset when the qualification was dropped within the early years' sector; suddenly rendering her incredible qualification completely useless – furthermore, unqualified - despite having a significant knowledge on play and successfully using it for the benefit of the children in her care, whilst also being the foundations of her children's learning.

Practitioners who have experience in Playwork are using their experience to enhance their children's day and practitioners who are using play as a main theme for learning, should develop their understanding of the deeper benefits of play so they are facilitating it better. Our role as early years practitioners is to follow the child's unique path of exploration and investigation through a Playwork Inspired Learning approach, whilst following the *Early Years Foundation Stage (DfE, 2017)*, and *Characteristics of Effective Learning (EE, 2012)*. We also use the Spice model *(Brown, 2014)* to ensure children develop using a whole child approach. The path is messy, and some children develop further in one area faster than others, an example of this is a child climbing a slide unassisted yet unable to speak fluently. Children all develop uniquely following their own path of learning, whilst working towards a curriculum-based set of outcomes.

Playwork is no longer taught in any modules within the early years curriculum for any practitioners who are training, and many practitioners are under the belief that Play and Playwork are the same thing. This could be due to the quotation *"play is the work of childhood" (cited in Saracho and Spodek, 1998)*, just like playschool has become pre-school, play is the work of the child, but in its pure uninhibited form, not used as a tool for teaching. Play has become diluted and misunderstood.

This approach works in conjunction within the *Early Years Foundation Stage (DfE, 2017)*, moreover, children reach and attain their outcomes faster and more naturally. This is achieved using compound flexibility *(Brown, 2010, p3-55), Ludocentrics (Else 2014, p76-79),* play cycles *(Else and Sturrock, 2003)* and Play spirals *(Moyles, 1989)*, along with many more Playwork and play approaches which have been adapted to suit children under five, which can be found in *chapter 4 – 'what is Playwork Inspired Learning.'*

I think now, you can better understand why the approach is called Playwork Inspired Learning. However, there are many other reasons than just the examples above and this chapter will help you to further understand the reasoning behind the name, the inspiration and how it works. Each component of the name is purposeful and carefully chosen to ensure there is no misunderstanding of what the main points of this approach is about.

It is also important to note that Playwork, rightfully so, has never been mentioned anywhere within early years. Therefore, I believed it needed introducing properly and acknowledged appropriately, which is why it became a priority to have it as the focal part to this approach - as it is the main part of this approach. In contrast to this, there is a lot of my own information and research from the last twelve years included. However, Playwork is the overarching principle for the purpose of this approach.

Playwork is brought into the title and is there because of the sheer amount of research that has been developed from that field. Traditionally, Playwork is kept within the realms of older childhood (years 5 - 12), but I have developed a lot of this theory for the benefit of younger children, which has not been done before. A lot of terms will be new, but working together through this book, you will realise what has been missing from early years and you will recognise just how important these theories really are. It is important to note Playwork is not educational and it does not promote teaching or planning. By creating these spaces for play as *cited by Lester (2017), "when Playworkers modify the space, add materials and respond to play cues they can explore what could be, imagine what could happen and what could become, just as children do when they play"*, what *Gale (cited in King and Newstead, 2018 p117),* calls *"an enquiry into the 'not yet known" (2014, p677).* It is based on what children do when they have all constraints removed and are just observed from a distance without adult interference while giving you an understanding to develop and see what the child can achieve without being encouraged or steered towards a goal. This is achieved with children of all ages working either separately or in a group to create whatever they desire, this is how children operate in their everyday lives, whether it be kicking a can along the road on the way to school or hanging around in fields and parks - literally anywhere adults are not present. This may not seem relevant right now, but it really is significant - this is play in its best form. You may get annoyed at the child kicking a can in the street but there is a psychological value in this which you will learn to recognise in this book.

Now you understand Playwork is for an older age group, this is where the *'inspired'* comes from. Any research I have used, I have changed it slightly to work with our age group, however it relates directly to Playwork; inspired seemed the most appropriate word to use. Playwork Inspired Learning envelopes the gap between formal learning and unreserved play - blending how the child is capable of learning without interruption and explaining, and showing you how to use it in conjunction with the statutory framework we must support.

Learning is something we do daily within our roles, whether it be early years or any educational sector, however, for the purpose of this book, I am focusing on children under the age of five. Learning is something children are doing from birth, regardless of whether it is the first time or the hundredth time, there is still something new for the child to learn. How the child learns is completely unique to the child, some will learn to walk before talking and others talk long before they walk. The journey is for the child to develop as and when they are ready to try things, rather than when it is believed the child is ready. Much like a book, if you skip chapters throughout the book, you miss small pieces of important information which usually means the finished book is incomplete as there are gaps in the plot. A child's brain is the same, there is a natural series of steps a child will take from birth to reach bigger milestones, if we encourage children to miss steps, there will be gaps in the child's development that will be missed which you cannot go back and correct easily.

Children learning to move, speak and reach new goals through their own experience has been something that has helped children develop without complete adult intervention for many years. Our drive to get them further ahead, walking, talking, counting or drawing, using *'paid for'* services are not always preparing children in a way they can easily learn; learning through repetition instead of allowing the child to learn through trial and error. Playwork Inspired Learning uses natural forms of play for the child, while they learn new ways and practice their own way of learning to move forward.

Play was not included in the title as it is bandied around everywhere, play has become a buzz word rather than a mysterious entity that belongs to the players - in this case, the children. As adults we play, it's a given rite that carried on from our own childhoods and stays with us as in the everyday jokes we tell, pranks we play, and every fence you touch as you walk along the road (I know I'm not the only one!) I have witnessed the term play being used as a word that people are embarrassed to use, I've seen play-school become pre-school, play being used as a tool to develop learning and play being used in a pre-planned format where the opportunity for genuine child driven play is limited. This is my opportunity to put play back in its place within the sector and promote this unique perspective of play using its own name as its driving force.

Playwork will help me justify the freedom of putting play back into the laps of the children, bring pride back into telling parents *'yes, we play!'* without immediately retracting and saying we learn through play, because play isn't about what we want them to learn, play is play - magical, enchanting, and a delight to watch. If given the right tools you will see learning from a whole new perspective, non-intrusive, hands off learning. You will develop skills on how to assess the whole child, i.e. spiritually, holistically and academically.

Before you shake your head and say I am crazy, give me a chance with this book to explain…

1. You want the children to play more and be brave using the word *'play'* as a concept that does not need the word learning attached to it. Play is the child's way of learning but is part of the process of playing.

2. During the lockdown of 2020, practitioners want to recognise the significance of play; as practitioners we need to understand what play can bring, therefore this approach will teach you how to enhance deeper level learning using Playwork.
3. We need to understand that play is a fantastic opportunity for children to learn for themselves through trial and error, rather than have play implemented by adults.
4. We do not need to interrupt play to make it something teachable (there are opportunities to do this, but this will be discussed later). Children that have opportunities to develop their own play have much better ideas in imaginative and creative play and learn to develop their language skills through practice with their peers.
5. Learning is natural, as is play - everyone does it, even adults!
6. Playwork and play are separate entities but can be used to complement each other rather than to work against each other.
7. There is an opportunity to give children skills for whole life coping strategies rather than key areas to prepare them for school readiness, hoping to impart life-long skills through careful observation rather than set tasks.
8. To save money, early years has the smallest budget of every sector - you don't need to buy equipment, stock or materials, nor redecorate the setting to use this method.
9. Develop the psychological understandings of play, why it is necessary and how you can develop an awareness of the child who is confident, self-aware, resilient, and prepared for not only school, but will cope in most situations.
10. Children will regulate each other! If they don't like something, they will develop their own voice in telling the child they aren't happy with what they see. If the child sees a child doing something they do not believe is safe or, what they think isn't safe - then you can guarantee the person doing the mischief making WILL be told by their peers! As practitioners, we have the fortunate position to be able to hear and see what is occurring and the children literally ask their peer at least twice before reporting it to an adult. Critically, the child doing the

telling has no idea that we have witnessed them trying - but come over with some pride to *'tell off'* their friend! We can then agree with them that they have done well trying and ask the child to listen to their friend - or we can suggest that the child may not have been very clear and accompany the child if they need support on developing ' *their voice'.*

Finally, you will be able to help the child achieve some milestones earlier than the *Early Years Foundation Stage (DfE, 2017)* and the *Developmental Matters (EE, 2012)*, by working in a different style and mindset than you are used to.

Research from my dissertation pointed these few struggles out from other practitioners across the United Kingdom, we all want the children to play more - inside and outside within their time with us. We all want the absolute best for our children, however, at this present time there is a huge gap. This is where I can show you change is possible, children will be better prepared, and our earliest years can only benefit from this way of being. The theories we use are outdated but still relevant despite now having technology in everyday life, education changes and reforms, and even family make-ups are different from the theoretical perspective they came from all those years ago. Some theories have been worked to ensure they have changed and adapted with time, such as *Steiner (1882)* and *Montessori (1907).* The new approaches that have been developed by practitioners have been exciting and transformative in how practitioners do their job. These have begun to show the difference modern methodology can impact on the way a setting works to enhance the child's time in childcare for a positive; such as In the moment Planning *(Ephgrave, 2015)* which removes the practice of the numerous pieces of paperwork for settings and the curiosity approach *(Bennett and Hellyn, 2019),* which uses older theory combined with their own to create a rich approach based around the children in their care.

We are moving away from stuffy environments where plans were created months in advance and were used at set times of the year, themes have also started disappearing within early years, with the exception of school based nurseries and reception year of school. We are making the right changes but Playwork Inspired Learning is transformative in psychological and physiological child development which focuses on the child's psyche, whilst having the ability to ensure they are learning their way, not how we anticipate or expect them to learn - think of it as the bowl which catches the jelly in a colander. We as practitioners focus on containing the jelly. The team is more relaxed, they have time to sit from a short distance away and observe and they also have more input in the setting and its workings which brings fluidity and calm to the children. It is a cycle of incredible transformation which can be felt by parents when they come into the setting; the children are also excited to join in and practitioners are adept at troubleshooting problems as they arise rather than inhibit creativity. It is important to note - the children do not become feral with a less hands-off approach and practitioners will work smarter and harder!

4

What is Playwork Inspired Learning?

This book is primarily for those within early years practice; however, it is also a useful resource for parents or anyone who has regular interaction with children under the age of five. I am however, planning on writing a book specifically for parents, because this book is based on larger groups of children, so is better suited to practitioners such as childminders, childcare on domestic premises and nurseries.

Children are sponges for learning between 0-5, neural pathways are developing at an incredible rate, therefore anything the young child learns during this time is crucial and will stay with them for the rest of their lives. We are the most important sector; helping to develop our future working adults, establishing relationships with children to prepare them for school, colleges, and future workforce. How we treat the children in our care will imprint these children for the rest of their lives and we need to ensure we treat the children in our care with the greatest of respect; despite this though, we are, for the large part, the significantly forgotten sector. Our roles are wide and diverse and the things we are expected to do in this sector keep increasing. Thanks to the research being developed by practitioners across the United Kingdom, there have been a couple of new developments and opportunities to play with real world equipment recently, and natural resources have been introduced too which can only improve children's opportunities.

Play has also become prevalent within early years, becoming the main themed process for learning. However, there is an obvious recognition within the sector that use of play is being used for something that it is not. Play is play and Playwork - up until now - has been a different field of study. Both play and Playwork have been mistakenly used as though they have the same meaning - which is untrue. They have links, but both are potentially being represented incorrectly within the early years community. Playwork Inspired Learning provides occasions where you can implement teachable moments, but this is done with limited interruption completely led by the child, rather than the adult. Playwork inspired learning develops deep psychological understanding from what the child is doing and explains what drives the child to do it, how it benefits their own learning and how to add this on the child's learning outcomes without impacting on the original intention of Playwork being non-academic.

Everything your child touches, engages with and interacts with is for a purpose to help them learn. They do not always necessarily need a helping hand from an adult; a child working or seeing something from another child may be the solution they are looking for. This approach may appear messy and in conflict with current approaches that may be used in your setting, but it is completely mindful of the child's ability to be able to do things for themselves and learn through trial and error guided by their inquisitiveness and their born desire to learn. Children learn how to manage their feelings when they *'learn they don't always win,'* and some things are just too tricky *'at the moment.'* Perseverance however, will always be a win for the child, and their confidence - despite being temporarily knocked - will soon come back with fighting spirit.

Have you looked at your setting and wondered how it works for the children, but they are too young to tell you the things they like and dislike? How do you know the children are having a good time and have opportunities to learn without having to keep *'teaching'* or moving on to the next step using planned outcomes to reach that one milestone it seems impossible to track within the *Early Years Foundation Stage (DfE, 2017)?* I will introduce you to new perspectives on how to assess areas that work and those that don't, and how you can change it around to make it work. Expanding on this, we will look at how things that appear to have a purpose to the children, even when things feel completely irrelevant; and how you can use this to your advantage - everything within your setting has a use, a purpose and an advantage to the children, you just may not see it yet.

Do you find you are inadvertently talking at the child rather than interacting, leading conversations, and steering them with questions, only for the child to suddenly lose interest quickly? Or do you find yourself trying to play with the children for them to direct everything though you, where you become the focus of the conversation - even though they were having a conversation with each other beforehand? Children do not always need to have an adult at hand to assist. This book will show you the benefit of how becoming a mindful observer of the children, can be more satisfactory than being a part of it. Unfortunately, our childhood and ability to play alongside the children has gone, grown out of us, which is why we do not understand why the children play the way we do and why random items are used for different things. Our imagination may be incredible, but you will never defeat the imagination of the child. Playwork Inspired Learning will show you how to be playful, yet mindful of other players and their own games safely, giving the children the opportunity to just get on. The only time you should stop play is if it becomes dangerous to others and even then, observation and knowledge of the child is paramount.

Do you wish your team had more time to relax and enjoy their role without feeling they need to be recording, working to fit in learning outcomes, working in small groups to achieve outcomes and run ragged trying to keep up with every child at all times (how we don't go cross eyed I will never know)? My working team have fun playing alone, chatting as a group and sometimes, playing away from the children! They are also amazing soloists on the dance floor and just as good with the maracas as the children. By showing the children we can have fun alone, they learn that it is acceptable for them to do this too - there is no pressure to do anything but have fun. We also have no room leaders within our areas either - this ensures a relaxed atmosphere where the team all know what they need to do but there is a time and a place for paperwork, which often includes children getting their own pen and paper and completing transition forms alongside the practitioner, anything the practitioners can do - you can bet your bottom dollar, the children will join in as well. The practitioners work as a team and therefore take ownership as a team when it comes to understanding the room and its dynamics. I am fortunate, that as an owner, I have relinquished almost all my office duties and can sit in the room along with the practitioners. When I am in the room, I am another practitioner, I do not need to tell the team what to do, they know their roles already and I am one of them - changing nappies, playing and having fun. If I am in the office (low picket fenced space just off the main room), the children will often come and ask me to come in (you see why I am safer outside the office!?). Children know who the players are, and they also know those that aren't, it is important the children know they are free to ask anyone to play. The practitioners work autonomously yet together like a well-oiled machine, if the practitioner has a headache or something similar, we as a team work together to protect them rather than make their day any harder - they came in, so are able to work, but they have lighter duties when it can be helped. What is fantastic and I really generally enjoy are the conversations children bring us into about our jobs. The children have no idea we are working and they certainly could not tell you who was in charge; when it does get mentioned, the children look at us practitioners to try and figure out who is. When they realise it is me, they look at me in disbelief! The children know who the adults are and know our job is to look after them, but rank means absolutely nothing to them - nor us.

Playwork inspired learning will also give you the ability to know your child better than spending one on one time with them and reading what others have to say about the child. Watching children at play will give you a sense of their general psyche and attainment at the precise moment the child is at play, safeguarding concerns are easier to witness during play, as the child is more inclined to play it out with another child rather than *'speak out'* or confide in an adult if they have become distrustful of other adults.

This new approach will open your eyes to things you have seen within your setting and enable you to understand why the child does things the way they do and how it is subliminal messages that can tell you how the child is, not just developmentally, but holistically too. When I started developing my approach over twelve years ago and recognised the benefit of working the way I do - my mind was blown. Once I started studying, I recognised I could attach my way of working to a modern theory; Playwork, and this opened my eyes further. This approach is a real game changer and could revolutionise the way everyone works with children.

The theory of Playwork is current and is in a constant cycle of being updated, evaluated, and developed. The use of adventure playgrounds, Loose Parts and natural environments for children has been developed within the last seventy years. In contrast to this, early years has been relatively underdeveloped over the last one hundred years. Many ideas for early years have been taken from Playwork, and have been tweaked to accommodate the use of young children within settings. An example of this is Loose Parts play *(Nicholson, 1971)*, which came into Playwork theory in the 1970's, where settings have made tinker trays and used small parts for children to make connections for fine and gross motor skills; furthermore, creating scenes and developing children's ideas based on their interests. There are lots of Playwork theories being used but not being acknowledged as being from Playwork backgrounds - therefore, Playwork Inspired Learning gives the credit back to the field it originated from, rather than trying to be anything else.

Playwork Inspired Learning uses the *EYFS (DfE, 2017)*, and Playwork theory to provide opportunities to create extra elements of working that benefit deeper level learning for the children in our care, creating and developing resilience, personal well-being and confidence for when our guys leave us to go to school. Instead of developing and creating play for the children, we watch the children develop and create their own play for their own outcomes when they are physically, mentally and developmentally ready.

Is Playwork something you are interested in, but now it isn't a relevant qualification for your role, so you feel it is pointless looking into? Have you studied Playwork and struggle to find a way to make it work in your setting? Did you learn Playwork as part of your studies, but you felt it wasn't made completely clear why it was so valuable? Are you not sure of the difference between play and Playwork and are intrigued by this? if so, this book will help you to recognise the power of Playwork Inspired Learning, using real life examples to link this approach to the *Early Years Foundation Stage (DfE, 2017)*, recognising you can use both with incredible results. Even if you use another theory within your setting, Playwork has such a massive part to play. Playwork Inspired Learning will slip in, even if just a little and the changes you use can transform a confident child into one that walks around with such pride, you can almost see peacock feathers as they show themselves off! You know you have helped the child for the whole of their lives. As adults, we have all been through some huge transitions and challenges we never anticipated happening, with this in mind we have the opportunity to equip children with the skills to give them a small step ahead to help them - we would be mad to not grab this opportunity!

We follow the *Early Years Foundation Stage (DfE, 2017)* in conjunction with the approach, however, it is recognised children develop faster using their own ability rather than the assumed outcomes of what they *'should be'* doing. The children are only split during primary pre-school hours as each group can define their core skills whilst using Playwork Inspired Learning to develop themselves. In contrast, the preschool setting, is attached by a door and is developed over four rooms defined by purpose i.e. construction,imagination, arts and crafts and reading room. These terms are more relevant for adults and visitors to the setting rather than the children - everything is transferable between rooms, and children have open access to all of these rooms during their day.

The following theory is used when children reach pre-school age and should be used occasionally when developing activities such as play dough, scissor skill and if the child wants to, to develop writing skills. It is important to acknowledge this theory, so it can be dipped into rather than be a main feature of Playwork inspired learning. Again, being heavily reliant on the room to enable choice rather than expecting it as a taught skill.

By developing rooms according to social and solitary play rather than age groups, children of all ages are enabled to interact and socialise whilst creating a *"Play Spiral" (Moyles, 1989).* A Play Spiral is a space created to encourage a free play space, where the child has an opportunity to learn for themselves. Critically, this theory suggests a child moves from needing child initiated play to requiring adult intervention to challenge the child into their next stage of personal development. The child is then left to develop from what they have learned from the adult in a spiral motion, this is a method used within many forms of child led provision, but is has to be done within a cautionary approach not to impede the child's own thoughts and ideas. Whilst the *"Play Spiral" (Moyles, 1989)* has many uses within the setting, intervening in the children's play is done very rarely and only if the child requests the adult to join in - furthermore, older children are usually asked considerably more often than adults. This can also stop the natural flow of play, causing play annihilation - where the game is over, and the players stop playing. There is a fine line between interrupting and taking over play to becoming a participant in the children's play. As previously mentioned, the setting wants children to play their own games, leading their own play for their own outcomes. By joining in without being asked, the play is transformed from something that was child led to something quite unexpected - an adult led activity, without realising. This theory is relevant in recognising children need space to develop their own skills, but does not give opportunity for practitioners to learn when a child should be left and when to intervene. As previously mentioned, children should be observed significantly more than they are led in their own play.

During half terms and after school, the children are together in the large open baby and rising two's room. There are many benefits to this and all age groups can learn significant lessons from everyone, for example, language, movement, conflict resolution as well as confidence and a feeling of self-worth. The eldest children have a feeling of being important and necessary as part of the setting as helpers within the setting, preschool children help encourage and enable the rising two's and play with the babies in setting too, which helps teach all of the children understanding, developing knowledge of other age groups and having opportunities to have open conversations about the things they do not understand. One of the loveliest examples I can think of was one of our children had just started the journey to reading but was not confident to read to everyone, however we told him the younger children did not know words and if he got it wrong, they wouldn't notice - he soon became quite confident in reading to the younger children which helped his confidence in learning to read to other age groups and even adults.

Early years development has developed slowly over the last ten years, with the current *Early Years Foundation Stage (DfE, 2017)* framework, focusing heavily on toilet training, speech and movement, rather than basic colour development, young children's ability physically and early development. Using tapestry we have the ability to log development regardless of age and ability, therefore when children are able to climb a slide for example, we can still log it, despite the child only being one year old; however, this *'outcome'* should only be met when the child is 36 months old. This is not only unfair on the practitioner who can *'prove'* this happened, but the child who cannot be held back just because the child should not be old enough. The use of Playwork Inspired Learning enables the child to develop this way naturally, by learning through example; in this case observing older children achieve goals and then trying these new strategies themselves to achieve the same goal.

Have you ever been bamboozled with huge chunks of information you struggle to understand, or feel like you aren't good enough to make sense of what is being said, but are afraid to put you hand up say you just don't get it? Having that feeling, that despite reading and re-reading, the information is still out of your comfort zone? This is where we can be friends! I have been given opportunities to speak at university, help many people set up business and help when colleagues are struggling to understand complexities within their studies. There is one thing that has always been brought up in conversation; how I talk and relay information. I may be hugely academic and yes, I may be experienced - the wealth of knowledge I have taken on and developed over the years is phenomenal - however, what I promise to give you is the opportunity to read a book unlike any book you have read before now. Yes, I could fill you with complex words and confuse you, or I could engage you and explain in layman's terms. Not only does it make the book more interesting if you struggle to take information in, but I will at least try and make you smile whilst learning the difficult stuff. Not only will you feel empowered, you will feel a satisfying feeling of already doing the right things but learning how to use this new power with ease. I promise not to bombard you with over complicated information (it kind of is, but it won't feel like it), I will speak to you like another person doing the same job as me - with a couple of qualifications to boost my approach.

It is important to add, there is also a lot of my own ideas contained within this book which also compliments how this approach works fully within my own setting. There is nothing that isn't tried and tested over the years, but I am honest when things have been tested and failed (for example - messy play - chapter 8), however, things change all the time and we have managed to work through it and find a way to make it work without impacting on the children or our ethos.

From now on in, I promise I will be authentically me, clear and honest. Rest assured, I can be academic if I have to be, but this approach to writing the book makes the approach accessible to everyone! If you met me in person - this book is a true representation of me.

5

Challenging The Status Quo

There are many challenges when trying something new for the first time, like riding a bike - you will have a few stumbles before you are competent at riding, this approach is the same concept. It will take a few times before you *'get it,'* but once you do, you will wonder why you have not used it before now. There are many things you have seen but not been able to explain to understand the deeper meaning behind them.

If I failed to take the opportunity to introduce Playwork Inspired Learning to the early years after thirteen years of dedicated study and passion that I have put into it, it would be a significant disaster to the children in our care. Even more considerably so since I have worked so many years to prove how it can work within our sector. Yes, Playwork isn't supposed to work, but the theoretical processes used are so very important, it would be a disservice to every child if it were not tried. Furthermore, Playwork as a module has been taken off early years training qualifications and it is no longer recognised as a full and relevant level three within the sector, however, it is my belief that it is critical within early years and by the end of this book, I think you will agree.

There was an article in Nursery World back in 2009 *"Playworkers struggle to implement EYFS,"* the article discusses how Playworkers found it challenging to use both Playwork and the *Early Years Foundation Stage (DfE, 2017),* due to the differing philosophies between the two practices. The fear within the article is that Playwork will disappear and education will take over within all out of school provisions, something that cannot and should not happen. In agreement with my main concern is the belief that Playwork could in fact compliment early years, yet the reality is - the divide between Playwork and the EYFS is getting wider. Perry Else, author of the book the *"the Value of Play" (Else, 2009),* agrees the value of play will be squeezed out of early years, whilst recognising the similarity between the words *"child centred"* but meaning two different things to each field.

The challenge as an early years practitioner is to make this transition to recognise the value of Playwork to make play, work. To work and recognise children's holistic development using modern ideas, developments in understanding the relevance of play, and geographies of the room to ensure children can use every area in a ludic format which builds children's confidence and sense of intrigue and imagination when approaching their own play. Sorry for throwing in the word Ludic, it means spontaneous and undirected playfulness *(Oxford English Dictionary 2008)*, you will learn to love this word, I am sure. Play and Playwork are not the same thing, again, this book will build your understanding of the difference between the two. If you are already a Playworker working within the early years sector, this book will also enable you to refresh and empower the people around you to fully immerse in this magical new approach that is Playwork Inspired Learning.

Have you been in the position where you have tried to explain play and become unstuck? I think we have all had the occasion where this has happened and suddenly, we question ourselves! Adult interpretations of play and adults' intentions are rarely connected; this includes the focus of play as a mechanism or scheme for learning - the two just are not connected. Children play for play's sake, and what is quite often the case, some *'well-meaning'* adults then translate play and use it to create and develop learning. Although a lot of the *Early Years Foundation Stage (DfE, 2017),* is achieved using play, children's play should not be interfered with in any form to develop learning. Adult developed and created play is not play at all, it is a vehicle to learning through a gentle well-meaning approach for encouraging children. Activities such as this should not be the be all for children as they shape and grow, these activities have outcomes that are pre-designed and pre-organised, therefore how can children then turn this activity into a self-driven and holistic activity, when the basis of it is learning? Playwork Inspired Learning is not planned and pre-designed, therefore it is an approach as fluid as children's play- it has no end and no specific beginning; it just happens. Learning is, therefore, a by-product of the child at play, rather than learning via any form of play.

The understanding of play and its complexities are what is perhaps what has made the word its own enemy. Furthermore, this could be the reason why people are always trying to brand it as something. *Helenka, (1956 cited in Brown,2010, p3)*, was correct when she describes it; *"The illusiveness of play as one of its greatest strengths, both paradoxical and ambiguous."* The ability to pin a meaning on children's play and completely understand it is based on our own childhoods, therefore, just like theories of past, the eye of the beholder is just as unique. In contrast, understanding play occurs *'just because'* is not a justifiable argument when indeed some parents are involved - this is where deeper psychological understanding needs to take place.

We are not trying to define the play, we are developing understanding of the benefits of it, which in turn will hopefully put the power back in play - Playworkers, Playwork programmes and the field of play- including my own qualification, protects play for children. The benefits of play are tangible to everyone in this field, which is why it has been so well developed. Older children (remember, Playwork focuses on children from five years old), can describe and explain their reasoning when within the walls of an adventure playground, or playing on the way to school, however, in contrast they probably don't even realise some of the things they are doing i.e. kicking a can whilst walking along the road, or walking along a wall - simply because they wanted to and didn't think anything more of it. Again, Playworkers have developed and recognised psychological areas that are awakened when children play, also understanding what is happening at a subconscious level for the child - this is enhanced by the children taking part, children aged above five are capable of saying what they are doing and what is driving them.

There is a difficulty of letting children playing without high supervision also; children who are watched from a distance are more inclined to *'get on'* with what they are doing, they build confidence in their own ability as there isn't an adult there to steer them or guide them in their learning, or to be there if they come across an issue that is easier to resolve with an adult within close proximity. Children are also more inclined to use different language when they believe they aren't within hearing distance, much like private discussions - practitioners are more inclined to have better conversations when they think no one else can hear them. Practitioners who are encouraged to sit and witness children at play, for example, sitting in a triangle formation, can observe the children in their care from every angle of the room. As far as the children are concerned they aren't being watched, however the opposite couldn't be more true- the observant practitioner learns from the beginning, that watching groups of children is a virtual impossibility when you work alone, yet as a group set of eyes, how you sit or stand in the room lends the best opportunities for observations of the children.

Children should only be stopped when the child is at risk of harm, however, this does not mean take the child away i.e. younger child climbing a slide, you know they can't climb up, get closer, ready to jump in if the worst happens, however do not intervene immediately - the child may just surprise you with their ability. I have seen children who are not able to walk, barely able to stand, yet completely in control of their bodies when standing on a 45-degree angle holding on the sides of a slide! Another child who was only just crawling also learned how to climb up the slide after watching a three-year-old take his socks off before embarking on his trip up the slide. We were surprised he pulled his socks off - let alone ascend the slide! We were close enough to help him if he fell, but ensured he had the opportunity to attempt it without seeing us, and giving us the eye (like they do when they want help), using us to help him up before he had the chance to go it alone - and succeed! In both of these cases, the children were so pleased to have succeeded in what they had set out to do, however, if there was close observation and the child was taken away from the slide because *'they were at risk,'* both of these children would have given up and used an adult rather than try for themselves. Opportunities such as this teach a child to be creative, resilient and make their own decisions, which greatly encourages their confidence in setting out what they want to achieve. As I said before, some children will hit the developmental outcomes sooner than anticipated using Playwork Inspired Learning, just because the child has the ability to learn for themselves without us adults *'thinking'* we are helping, when unfortunately, the reality is, we are taking away opportunities due to assuming the child either, cannot do it, or needs us to help achieve what they are trying to on their own. This can lead to the child feeling the need to rely on adults to achieve what they want to do rather than relying on themselves, which can inhibit their sense of self-esteem, self-confidence and self-worth. You may feel that it is the nice thing to do but, in most cases, it's unnecessary. Stepping back enables the child to think critically and assess how to do it - if they are really stuck, they will either ask a friend (which is the normal case), or they will ask an adult. If the child needs someone else to help, next time they may be able to do it alone. As previously mentioned, there is a fine line between helping and taking over.

This deeper psychological approach will help you to understand play from this perspective whilst enabling you as a practitioner to give the children better and more opportunities for them to develop their own play, at their own pace and let this evolve naturally through observation rather than direct involvement. In all honesty, it will look like you are doing less as you become a mindful observer, however, the reality of Playwork Inspired Learning, means you will in fact be doing double the work for double the pleasure and you'll have much more fun and laughter than before.

Are you now feeling a little confused as to how you will use deeper level learning following different types of psychological processes, when it literally makes little difference to the children and their learning? Let me prove you wrong! These are small changes and anonymous changes, but it's these changes that will transform your setting from a learning environment to a playful one, where learning happens to take place. This change of thought process will be the significant awakening you have been waiting for, and you will not have needed to change a thing within the setting!

I know you think I am probably teaching you to suck eggs but this really isn't the case, this is just a small snippet of what this book will teach you - there will be a large proportion of information that is coming up that will overwhelm you, so it makes better sense to wean you in gently. Sometimes, I think it's good to remember why we do these things and what the benefit is outside the realm of the *Early Years Foundation Stage (DfE, 2017).*

At present Playwork is not recognised within early years, however, the more people are aware of it, the better, not only for the children we have now, but for the future generations. We are making moves in the right direction now reception years can enable children to have the freedom to move and learn whilst playing, but there is still a lot of time dedicated to teaching. By giving children the opportunity to learn this way, to then have them sit in classes just a year later seems strange but obvious, as children have a lot of curriculum based learning to do, however, children are so much more playful than we give them the ability to be inside school. More and more development has been implemented into play, such as forest school and scrap stores for use within school time. Children need more than one hour of time for play and playfulness - therefore, some children play the fool in the classroom, which critically, they can be penalised for. Boredom or not understanding can play a huge part, so it cannot be right that children should be restricted in their movement for as long as reasonably possible; our youngest children, their psychology and their spiritual development should be encouraged from birth. My belief of Playwork currently being ignored within early years - is that it has not been fully explored until now. When I was studying and developing this area, there were only two books within the university that mentioned Playwork and early years in the same book - one discussed them as separate entities and the other recommended it as unsuitable. However, as my practice is early years, I have worked unknowingly with Playwork for years and I have proved this information to be false.

Depending on how you record observations for each child, the opportunity should be as raw as the activity you observe. Each moment a child creates, will never be recreated in the same format again, therefore the snapshot of what the child is doing should be treated as such. If you cannot write it, do not try and *'back date'* or re-run the event in your head, memory is not always clear, and the opportunity may have passed. To prevent this happening, the practitioner always has a tablet or piece of paper in hand to record the event as it happens. Then there is no opportunity to second guess or make value that does not exist. Children are never aware of photos or videos taking place as this can also detract from what happens (camera phones and *'cheese!'* have become the norm), therefore every child loves to pose then they know there is a camera on them. Critically, Playwork Inspired Learning means there are significantly more observations that can be taken of the child, so I do try to limit the number of observations. I think the most we had logged in one day was 32 observations with 12 children in a setting - it is a little excessive! If your setting is pen and paper based, ensure you carry a notebook and pen in hand ready to write the glimpses of magic you see happen throughout your day, again, trying to remain true to what you see, rather than trying to fill gaps that you aren't 100% certain you saw. Staged photos serve no purpose as these are not playful moments, these are purposeful photos that interrupt and can change the outcome of the game - if you want to capture these types of staged photo, then give the camera to a child, they will not only relish this moment but will also teach them so many things about themselves and others. Another fascination is facetime! If this is possible within the setting, the children will either go silent or tell their own story.

To save filling out sheet upon sheet of paper for planning, we use a simple bubble/web chart to say what the children have done every day. This is collated and developed with the team around the end of the day, we take the main themes and how the activity has continued and developed. There are no links to the *EYFS (DfE, 2017),* there are no names added, next steps and no planning; at the end of each week we start a new sheet. This is a great way to see what the children are doing when other practitioners have been off or what things the children are enjoying currently. We also include the things children are talking about, e.g. paw patrol play in the kitchen area, or a song being requested on Alexa. We have these stored and filed away and they have enabled us to see what items children are genuinely interested in and if a toy has gone out of fashion with the children. The practitioners recently installed a hairdresser's area in the setting as children began using blocks and play cutlery as hairbrushes as well as the pre-existing hairbrushes. They installed a mirror and a table, and added hair-bands, clips, a hair-dryer (that didn't work) and the children spent many sessions brushing my hair, the other children's hair, and developing some lovely (if not painful at times), hairstyles. This, produced moments for children to discuss going to the hairdressers, adding gel to finished hairstyles and really encouraging discussions. After a month, the area was disbanded, and the table moved to the kitchen space. However, the children still use the mirror on the wall to check out their hair and facial expression - some children have also used the mirror to have conversations with each other via the mirror!?

For those practitioners who thrive on messy and mucky areas or running themes towards a topic, Father's day, being one of them, it is possible for activities to be set up, but children should be free to create their own work rather than just stamping a foot and cleaning up - if a footprint or hand-print needs taking, enable the child to develop this afterwards. Wiping it off straight after, does not give the child (especially babies), any opportunity to explore what substance they have had put on them. This could lead to children not liking mess and becoming tactile defensive (a strong dislike for any type of texture on their hands, such as shaving foam, paint or even water play). Everything in the setting should be the child's choice, if they choose not to be involved then this should be their right, and should not be argued, although, if the child wants to watch what is happening - this should also be a choice. This is how children learn to understand that their voice and opinion counts.

Children's opportunity for choice not only develops confidence in their opinion, resilience and coping strategies when faced with things they are not sure of, but also strengthens them holistically. Not only is this important within Playwork Inspired Learning, but also within the *EYFS (DfE, 2017), Development Matters (EE, 2012),* and the *United Convention for the Rights of the Child UNCRC (2014), under Articles 5 - "Respect the rights and responsibility of parents and carers to provide guidance to their child as they grow up. This must be done in a way that recognises the child's increasing capacity to make their own choices", Article 12 - "the child has the right to express their views, feelings and wishes in all matters affecting them, and have their views taken seriously", Article 13 - "Every child must be free to express their thoughts and opinions and to access all kinds of information", Article 29 (goals of education) - "education must develop every child's personality, talents and ability to the full", Article 31 - "every child has the right to relax, play and take part in a wide range of cultural and artistic activities" (Unicef, 1989).*

Why should you follow Playwork Inspired Learning when play and playing isn't a main theme of the *Statutory Framework for the Early Years Foundation Stage (DfE, 2017)*? Well, this is something I can honestly say I don't know. I use the two in conjunction with each other and meet more outcomes this way than primarily developing children ready for school. Children have access to everything discussed in the framework, however we achieve these outcomes in slightly different ways. As we all agree, we all work uniquely but towards the same goal, therefore this approach is like other theories but aligns different areas of development to over-arch the key themes or seven areas of development. I will say seven now, because children from birth are exposed to all areas for development, the entire setting can work with all the areas so it doesn't make sense to only work with the prime areas, when the specific areas are accessible.

The benefit of introducing Playwork Inspired Learning to your setting is monumental! The theories being used within this approach are no more than fifty years old, whereas traditional early years theory is based on theorists from at least one hundred years ago - this point alone screams at me! Half the technology that exists now did not exist in any theory from back then - children do not have the same family make up and society is also completely different. Yes, it may still be relevant, but how, as an early years professional, can you not recoil with horror with the fact that children as young as three are now being diagnosed with depression!? There is something terribly wrong and we must act fast to change this at both setting level as well as higher, however - I am only one setting. I have championed this type of work for many years and have strived to ensure anyone I speak to can understand this difference - it has always left people asking questions and intrigued. Many people have been perplexed that I have not just written a book, surprised that I have pushed to be as qualified as I can. Others have encouraged me to speak, just because (if you cannot tell), I am enthusiastic but explain things in a fun light-hearted way.

6

The Proof Is In The Pudding

We have discussed the misunderstandings and opportunities of Playwork Inspired Learning, now it is time to introduce how to bring it to life in your place of work. This chapter will give you examples of how it is used and how to use it yourself with no impact on your current practices. Again, this is more of a psychological approach rather than a physical approach. This chapter will discuss how to use theory within your setting to make it more playful for the child, without impeding on the children in your care, yet implementing the *Early Years Foundation Stage (DfE, 2017).* It will also provide feedback from parents who use my service and what they think of this form of learning.

Let us start with some feedback from parents, these children have now left and gone to school, so you can see further ahead than just my early years provision!

"My little girl joined Little Monsters when she was 10 months old, following a fantastic settling in time, she was off to a flying start. She stayed with them until she went to school. What Chris has created here is not just a childcare facility, it is a home away from home, where staff become friends and children learn, love and grow. I would frequently pick Evie up and come in to join in with the fun play times, through her constant ability to choose her own play in a safe environment, it has given her an excellent start to primary school with her regularly receiving compliments and stars for her ability to play and share with others, look after her friends when they are hurt or struggling (one girl got very upset when she couldn't do her coat up, Evie stepped over gave her a cuddle, calmed her down and then started the zip for her and let her finish it off!) Being at Little Monsters gave her the tools to learn how to socialise,

empathise, care and learn without realising she is learning. She still tells us now that 'sharing is caring', and despite having left a year ago, she still talks about her time at Little Monsters and the fun things she would do. The basis that Chris has provided is exactly the same ethos that we are using at home, any opportunity to have fun is an opportunity to learn. With the ability to choose what she does and to discuss with friends, she continues a very firm friendship with 2 girls that have gone on to the same school and continues another friendship with a girl who doesn't go to the school. I truly believe that the foundations created by Chris are what has supported her becoming such a bright, friendly and kind little girl."

"The choice of setting for one's own children in the modern world is one fraught with stress. The desire for the child to be carefully nurtured and cherished is natural, but also to be allowed the space to learn to develop into a functioning person. We visited many settings but the child-led, play based ethos was so thoroughly and entirely engrained within all of the activities in the setting that the decision for us was easily made. It was clear to see that children were allowed the space – physically and emotionally – to develop at their own pace, with observations being made to inform and guide this rather than being a means to their own end. The children are not unnecessarily interrupted from their learning to follow pre-defined adult timetables, and the space was clearly designed for the benefit of children rather than the convenience of adults. The end result was confident, socially adept children who are ready to learn within other environments and for that I cannot thank Chris enough."

How do you start?

Check out the layout of your room - the layout shows how inviting it is to adults not so much the child, it looks amazing doesn't it? Okay, now invite a child in and see how the child views the space. Lefebvre's theory of spaces

(Cited in Pipertone, 2019), develops the role of the spaces which we use and how they could be perceived differently for anyone that uses them, what practitioners see when they set up the room, what visitors observe and toys they see, and what children envision are completely unique to the person; it is a perceptive space. This can be explained with the following example - a parent comes to look around and sees an empty box and thinks *'mess'* or assumes we just haven't thrown it away yet. The practitioner sees many opportunities and considers it to be useful for something like an art project or to use it to develop role play. However, the child sees endless opportunities and can use it considerably more creatively for endless opportunities. As heard on the television - one person's trash is another person's treasure.

The room is a geography of the space for the child, how they use and manipulate areas of the room should be up to them and their ability. Predefined does not always mean pre-determined, it has been created and developed for a purpose in mind, rather than for the child, however, the child should have the flexibility and opportunity to use the space how they wish. Unfortunately, as early years practitioners, we have to have a setting that has to meet guidelines for learning; whether your setting is 100% natural, a blend of both natural and plastic, or even following any specific approaches - there is always a time for play. Just like parks and playgrounds have a purpose as a space for children to develop, your setting is the same, it is an adult designed space for a child's use. As we all know, children prefer to climb up slides and we as adults probably remember laying down on the roundabout, playing drop an item then first to pick it up wins...We had the ability to be just as creative, but this does not mean we should interfere with how children play now.

Room leaders

Why do we feel that we need one person to lead the room? When working towards a calmer and happier space for the children and adults alike, we should be working in a co-constructed setting. Each practitioner comes with their own set of skills and these should be what drives the room. In my setting, we have practitioners who are fabulous at creative, messy and outdoors play. Using these key skills as a team, rather than putting one person in charge, ensures that all practitioners have a voice and take part ownership of their space, it also means when they want to make changes, they can - after all, they work long hours in this space, so should at least feel comfortable in it. By having no specific member of the team *'running'* the room, everyone ensures to work together to ensure all paperwork is achieved as a team. This changes the dynamic of the room, even when I work in the room, I am another member of the team - the children have no idea who is in charge, which is as it should be. Children under five do not need a hierarchy of staff working with them, we should be operating as a professional extended family caring for the child because that is our role, not person specific roles depending on what level of the chain we are on. This includes deciding breaks as a team, as well as any trips out or festivals the team want to create things for, again, on the understanding - only if the child wants to.

The first thing visitors notice when they come to the setting is the relaxed atmosphere; the practitioners are relaxed talking or busy observing the children, the children are also relaxed as they are busy doing exactly what they need to do and therefore are usually engaged in their own play, rather than recognise there is a stranger in their room. Quite often, I have a child come to join me, they just come along and hold my hand or ask to be picked up, they are not distracted away and don't very often talk, but they will happily hold my hand and enjoy the experience - this is their space so I'm not surprised they want to come and see what is happening. The children and practitioners recognise our practice brings fluidity and functioning to anyone that views the setting - each person within the setting sees exactly what they want to see. The setting has been solely designed for the use of children, this is recognised by *Russell (2013)*, recognising the need for children to *"appropriate their own lived space,"* while the setting remains unchanged during the time children are not present, when children are in setting, they have the flexibility to change the setting as they wish bringing *"certainty and uncertainty, repetition and difference" (Russell, 2013, p45).*

Key person

As early years practitioners we all understand our responsibility and our roles in creating caring roles and relationships with the children, this is still a priority within our setting, however, children often flit between who their favourite person is. Just as children do at home with their parents, suddenly liking one parent more than the other - then there are favourite grandparents too! Children recognise what different practitioners can offer and go to them for different needs on different days. Working with this in mind, the children have fixed key workers for their development, however, when the child first starts, the person they bond to first, becomes their key person. As the child grows, they have flexibility in who they go to for cuddles and rough play, however, they are not stuck to whomever they choose. This is good for children's confidence and instils trust in whoever they feel they need care from for their own needs. Not only is this beneficial to the adults who can care and spend time with whoever they want, the child then builds firm relationships according to their own needs. Again, when it comes to writing developmental plans, transition forms and recognising SEN issues, the whole team know the child from different perspectives, regardless if they were in or off for holiday or sickness. This ensures all paperwork is covered thoroughly and any gaps can be discussed depending on what other practitioners have observed during their time. Observations of the children are also completed as a team, so the key person has a multitude of different perspectives of the child and their development.

What is the difference between child led and child driven play?

There are many differences between children playing and other forms of playing in the early year's sector. Children and their opportunities for *'free play'* is also one full of holes for children really becoming involved and spending time raw playing. It is easy to tell the difference once you learn to recognise the difference. A child who has complete control over their learning will spend some time playing alone, then start to engage others in their play, before it becomes a group play session. Children who are able to drive their own play have opportunities to turn the game around in their actions and swiftly move from one idea to the next, child driven play is uniquely about the children meeting their own needs for play, rather than clear cut and defined play. Observations of children engaged in child driven play are blurry and not about the child stopping to look at the screen as you do not want to impact on what they are doing. Children will boss each other around, tell each other off and yet work as a group to play, and if one child gets upset or annoyed they will resolve the issue together, or they will come to the practitioner for support. Practitioners will be the unseen entity for children as they continue to do what they want within the space, with the only times a practitioner interrupts the play being to change a dirty nappy, to stop fights becoming physical and at meal times. Play which involves a practitioner will inherently become a different type of play built on expectation and rules whilst children interact with each other. Activities such as celebration cards are directed to meet parent's pleasure and practitioners have an idea of what they want to achieve - this does not involve the child until they have to do what they are asked to. Children, as much as they're clever little bugs, do not spend hours planning and organising these activities for their parents, and realistically we aren't really doing it for the children - so what difference does it make and how can you make this child driven? This question is answered further down, but hopefully it gives you a quick insight to what opportunities we are giving children according to what we ask of them.

An example of ensuring children have choices regardless of practitioner position can be seen from my own perspective. I do not like guns, I never have and therefore will not buy toys that are gun shaped. In my opinion, you cannot do anything but shoot people with a gun, therefore it is not something I want to introduce. However, in complete contrast - if the child has the imagination and drive to build a gun using the tools and equipment available to them then this is completely fine by me. The child has the imagination and confidence to build it for their own right, therefore I am not at liberty to put my personal feelings about this kind of activity on them. The children are aware that if they want to play guns, then they cannot shoot people that don't have guns. The children that want to participate extend their own game by making targets and can use equipment in the room to duck and hide from each other, children are so used to this way, they do not even need to be asked; going off to do this unprompted and respecting of others, usually asking other children if they want to play. This example shows, although my opinion may be different to the children - I respect their roles as the players feeding their own wants and desires through the purposeful use to make their own play. My perspective of the guns only being used to kill people is not the same as what they children may believe and it is not my place to push my feelings on them.

You can tell whether a child wants to participate or is scared by something they have been asked to do as well, children who are using their own drive are excited at the opportunities they are doing by themselves, you can easily tell the difference in photos too. A child who has been put in a tree is scared and fearful in photos, whereas a child who climbed up themselves would be happy and their body language would show a little fear, but the excitement would be the overarching expression. Children who are being led into situations they are not completely confident in, will display this in their body language and the things they say whilst they are doing it. The youngest children who are keen to try something new, such as an obstacle course, should want to try it rather than being put in the situation - this helps them build up their self-confidence and the trust in the practitioners who will only help them rather than put them in situations where they can become fearful and conflicted. Children who are eager to participate in an activity that has been set up should be given the opportunity to try before anyone starts to interfere with how they do it - only giving support when asked and only giving the support the child wants rather than completely molly coddling them and shielding them from making mistakes. There was another experience given to me by an old school friend, her child had literally climbed the washing pole in her garden! He was three years old and his mum could not find him - there he was, around 20 feet in the air, happily with his legs clenched tight and arms holding him still! She was absolutely horrified at this, but she didn't realise he could do this until it was already too late! Children will only do things they are ready to do, regardless of whether we want them to or not! Now I am not saying as practitioners we should enable a child to climb washing poles, street lights or such like; however, if a child is ready to push themselves, we should take a cautious step back and enable them to. Forest schools enable children to use hammers, sit around fires and to really engage with their whole physical being, therefore this should not be a fearful opportunity for the children in our care. Quite often, when I am using saws, screwdrivers, hammers and other tools, the children will ask to have a turn, which I will encourage, simply for the fact - not only do their parents do this at home, but we can teach them how to safely use these tools. Children love being part of an *'adult'* experience, therefore why not? These children will grow up willing to try new things and experiences, whilst learning health and safety, body positioning, and develop better hand-eye coordination - let alone the implications for their spiritual and holistic growth. Just like sitting down to write reports and notes about children (the endless tracking and developmental sheets), children will want to be included, the more opportunities they witness, the more interested they become in wanting to join in.

At Halloween, you take your child to go and pick out a fancy-dress costume to wear during the evening of the 31st, you purchase it and take it home. When the big day arrives, you dress the child up and out you go.

The child picked the fancy-dress therefore it is adult led (you took them), but as the child picked the costume, it is child driven. However, did the child have explicit freedom to choose or did you point out the boys/girls section? This makes it become adult led and child led.

When it came to getting ready, did the child go and put the costume on without being asked (as they had probably done every day since you bought the costume home) or had it been hanging in the wardrobe waiting for you to get it out and help them put it on? This is not an activity you would normally do in setting; however, it serves as a good example of the difference. If the child had been trying to put the costume on from the minute you got it, the costume was available and the child paid huge interest in it, then this is child driven. If you put it away and only gave them the costume to put it on specifically for the purpose of going, then this is adult led. The difference between the two is apparent, one is for the purpose of going out and the parent wanting the child to put it on, whereas the child putting it on for the sake of wanting to wear it, means this is completely child driven.

Another example, from inside the setting could be described as this;

The children, without prompting, set up their own game of duck, duck goose. The children are sat in a line, going round doing their 'duck, duck goose' thing, but one child starts to mess about - when he isn't chosen he starts to throw things. The other children aren't bothered by this and carry on their game, all the children are taking turns and playing the game following their own rule of running around their line of friends several times before going to sit down. The children are laughing, cheering their friends on and ignoring the child throwing things because it isn't impacting on their game - however, once the ball hits another child, he is quickly reprimanded by his friends who tell him to stop it or he wouldn't get picked. The practitioner that spots this play cycle in action then goes and tells the other practitioners what is happening and to join in the observation. One practitioner who does not like seeing the child throwing things as he is not following the rules of the game, goes and tells him, he can no longer play as he isn't joining in properly and spoiling the other children's play. The practitioner then decides she wants to take an observation of the children playing their own game they made up, so she goes and asks them to look in one direction so none of the faces are visible in the photo - so they stop playing and pose for a photo. When the photo is taken, children start getting up and the game is over, despite it being in full flow before it is interrupted. A few minutes after the child is told he can re-join his friends; the game had been forgotten about and they had grouped off in other directions. However, the children slowly re-start the game that had been abandoned and it resumes like it had not stopped. Again, there were no rules put in place by the children or the adults and the game continued smoothly as there were no interruptions.

From this example, the children playing had this game under control, they had told the child throwing things that he would not be included, and the child continued to do so, therefore he did not get picked. The children were taking turns and they were all happy playing - the minute the practitioner stepped in, the game was effectively over. Their own rules were not trusted, nor was their judgement. The game was stopped for a photo mid flow, which meant the children forgot who was running, who was chasing and who was probably next in turn (these are only assumptions). The minute the practitioner tried to give the game back to the children, their game had become abandoned, their own established rules were not accepted by the practitioner, when they should have been, and the children lost the joy they originally had. It took a long time for the children to re-establish this game, but the original playfulness this game had, was gone.

When referring this to the *Early Years Foundation Stage (DfE, 2019)*, the children were meeting their own learning objectives by playing this game, whilst staying safe and having fun. The children, who were ranged between 2-4 years of age (just about to leave for school), slowed down for the smaller, younger children and the older children went slower for the smaller ones chasing them, a couple of the children, who had not played this game before, were gently introduced to it without question and time was given to them to help them understand the rules in place. Another of the children who seemed to have no idea of what was happening, ran around them in circles while everyone carried on playing around them. Again, he was not stopped or penalised, the children just accepted he was going to run around alongside them and with them, yet not part of the game.

It may be quite nice for you, should you desire, to research the outcomes the children met within this game - this way you can start learning to judge an observation and its outcomes rather than outcomes expected. You could even, switch this up and try a planned game of duck, duck goose in your setting, writing out your anticipated expectations and contrast these to what happens when you walk away from the children playing, and let them take it over. However, if you have set this game up and walk away, you have still initiated this play, which in turn means adult initiated, and child led. You just have to be mindful to let the game play out, including new rules, children disrupting the game and unless it gets physical, ensure you position yourself away from the children so they think they are playing this game alone. This would only have been a truly child driven activity if they had created it by themselves without any prompting from adults.

Development

Tracking children's development is done by observations. Children are watched throughout their day, what they are playing with and what their ability is, is noticed. Children are around children of all other ages, up to the age three during term time and up to school age during half terms. The children learn by watching other children and their movements throughout their day. We have babies who are climbing slides during the day, learned by watching another child taking off their socks and going up the slide - younger children recognise this is how they can achieve the same. Younger children who don't yet have the ability to remove their socks will still try without as much success, but the other children encourage them to keep trying. This non interventional approach encourages older, i.e three and four-year-old children, to pay close attention to their younger friends, which in turn increases confidence in the children's ability, self-confidence and self-awareness. The youngest children i.e. 0-2 then develop resilience as they try and muster the confidence to push themselves harder to achieve.

Children soon get bored of the adult voices and we become a blur, which is understandable - no one likes a nag. Therefore, by only intervening when necessary, the children pay attention when the adults speak, as they know there is a value to our voice. This approach works for all children, not just sibling groups, as children universally enjoy the company of other children, so it makes sense to give older children the opportunity to develop their own skills rather than implementing on the children. Not only does this work for general play, this works for communication and language skills, and also cooperative play. Children are far more inclined to discuss strange and wonderful ideas when they believe they are not in the company of adults, practice language skills as they can use them on children that will not question them when they mispronounce words in a book, or have general chit chat. Children that have come from social services, or are under the care of social services, often take slower steps in building relationships with adults therefore, having the opportunity to build safe relationships with children is a far more holistic and *'safe'* way for children to build their confidence. Through their observations of interactions between the adults and the children - they learn to understand we are safe people worth trusting, rather than forcing a child to build a relationship with adults as a priority.

Children that are exposed to this type of care, build strong relationships with other children as well as the people who provide the care for them. Not having adults pushing relationships within the setting, teaches the children resilience and coping strategies greater than relationships that are built via adults working to establish the children and friendship circles. This helps the children learn how to develop relationships with others using their own confidence and ability - these relationships are also based on mutual respect rather than requirement, and more often than not continue into school.

The Play Cycle

The Play Cycle *(Sturrock and Else, 2009),* is recognised in Playwork, but is also inherent in early years, however, this is not always understood or recognised. Understanding this concept of play helps establish why play starts but can stop almost as fast. It also explains why children get so engaged in solo play, why the child takes interest in certain toys and objects (or us adults), and how to recognise it.

The easiest way to introduce the play cycle is this example; if you were walking along a road and you saw a metal fence (if you're like me!), it's quite nice to let your hand run along the fence (obviously without prickles in the way), feel the bumping under your hand, and if you are really lucky, you can hear the dull thud under your hand as it runs along. When the fence runs out, you put your hand back down and carry on as if you had never touched the fence in the first place.

Okay, so you may think I am mad, or you may be secretly nodding your head in the knowledge that you also do this! Now to explain why we do this, with little to no recognition that it is actually happening. This is what is known as a play cycle - when you see the fence (this is going to sound strange), the fence is offering a play cue (an invitation to play), by running your hand along the fence, you are accepting the cue to play. You accepting the invitation creates a play return, your actions and the fence making the funny noise and strange sensation on your hand is the cycle in action (the cue and return working together). When you reach the end of the fence, the game is over, this is known as play annihilation - the play cycle has come to a natural end as the fence has stopped. How does this relate to children though? Well, everything in the setting has an opportunity to create and develop a play cycle, like you have discovered, children that are given opportunities led by themselves have much richer and inviting areas to engage with. Through careful observation from a distance, you can see the play cycle happening everywhere - some only lasting a minute or so, then others starting to develop and gradually extended into other areas and absorbing many other items that creates a constant flow of a play cycle. All children have this ability and like us adults, we are quite often unaware of it taking place as it is a subconscious process. However, once you see it begin - there is a snowball effect that can stay as a solo game, a game which engages others or a game that can play out for an hour. It is important to note, that as practitioners we can quite often annihilate this play cycle without recognising it. Whether we join in and change the game to suit our needs which means children lose interest or we stop play to tidy up without warning. By introducing a playful environment where children have the opportunity to create and play out their own ideas, the play cycle can flourish, and children can lead and initiate their own play. This in turn, will develop children's resilience and well-being. That being said, I know I haven't mentioned the *Early Years Foundation Stage (DfE, 2017),* however, once you recognise the play cycle within the setting, the ability for children to move around freely within the setting and enabling the children to move things around the setting as part of their cycle, you will see the early years outcomes appear before your eyes. As an example of this, a child who had just learned to walk was carrying a metal saucepan in his hand whilst trying to manoeuvre around the room. As he reached the tiled end of the flooring he tripped and the pan clattered to the floor, as the child landed, instead of being upset, he really enjoyed the sound of the pan hitting the floor. He then sat himself up and carried on making a huge racket on the floor with the saucepan, however, after a few minutes of bashing, he got up and walked over to the plastic climbing frame and gave the saucepan a good bash against it. The little boy then went around the room experimenting with different sounds the saucepan made against different things, having the time of his life, undisturbed and learning for himself without having to create a group music activity for him to learn about sounds and noises. From this, it is clear the child learned in his own time through experimentation, yes it was noisy and a practitioner could have easily stopped it, but when given the opportunity to develop it himself - he learned how to change and create different sounds that were available to him, whilst building his own confidence, concentration and strategies to learn.

The above activity was about the child learning without being taught or adult engagement, no one had to plan this - his activity developed from a simple fall and a play cycle was developed. *Else (2009)* recognises children can build resilience and their own well-being without the need for adult support or pressure. However, in agreement with *Else (2009),* the play cycle does not mean learning is not taking place - you just have to recognise it. Some play takes place simply *'just because'*. Children are developing spiritually in Playwork Inspired Learning, as well as developmentally, but crucially, children are doing it their own way rather than playing for the purpose of learning - as previously discussed, learning is a by-product of play. Not playing to, playing for or learning through - play is play and learning is learning. Playwork Inspired Learning is watching the play and learning to recognise the learning taking place.

Connecting play to learning without play annihilation or teaching

Building from the last example of the play cycle, I am beginning to sew the seed of how to use Playwork Inspired Learning - where play isn't anything other than play, observations and children playing (and noise). If we apply a more hands-off approach, children can stimulate and encourage themselves and each other to learn. From children falling and accidentally learning about sound and experimentation, to the child who learned how to climb the slide by seeing other children, you are beginning to develop understanding on how children are learning all of the time. Just as children cannot be forced to drink or eat, children cannot be forced to play if they do not want to. Play is natural and involuntary, therefore, why shouldn't it be allowed to be the driving force within early years? *Brown (2006)*, discusses the use of Psycholudics (psycho - the mind, ludic -at play). This is another significant Playwork process that is inherent to Playwork Inspired Learning. Children's minds are always in a state of play, everything is and has an opportunity to be playful, its ensuring they have that ability. If you choose to set up an activity for the children, it is key to enable the children to only *'find'* the activity rather than be told there is an activity set up. This will encourage the child to naturally look in the area if they know there are things available within a set space. For us, messy play is always available to the children, there is playdough, glue and tissue paper, pencils and pens, however, on occasion, paint is put out for the children to really get creative without paint bombing the setting. With children having the free access to everything, you are engaging with their natural inquisitiveness and ludic behaviours to offer them new opportunities, if they investigate the area fully.

The children soon start Chinese whispers and tell other children about it, again, giving the children confidence and the ability to encourage or enable others. If they are confident enough to want to go and explore, their confidence will grow and as they paint with freedom and flexibility they develop resilience and self-assurance in their work. If a practitioner accesses the area the children naturally become talkative, discussing what they are doing, what they are intending to do and what they want to create, however, the practitioner ensures they do not steer or guide the child at work. Children need unstructured and self-defined play, the opportunity to make mistakes and get bumps, to not be under the constant supervision of adults and to be able to interact with children in their own way. Our role as practitioners is to observe and protect children from harming themselves or getting into situations which put them at significant risk. If Playwork works for children over the age of five, why should it not work for children under this age? They are still children; albeit body language becomes more important than physical language, interactions can be more challenging, and observations become more of a challenge. However, in return, children are

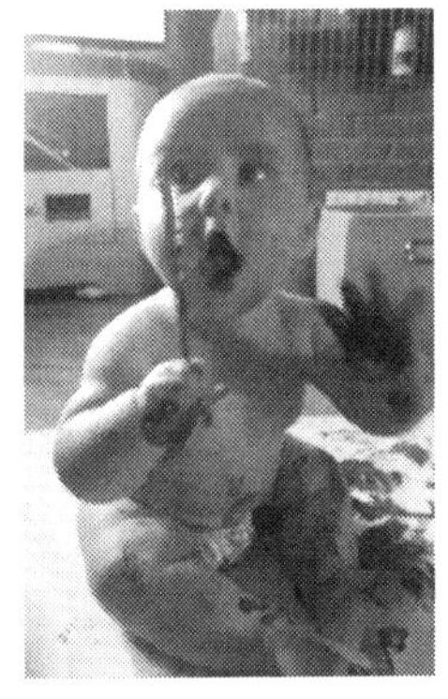

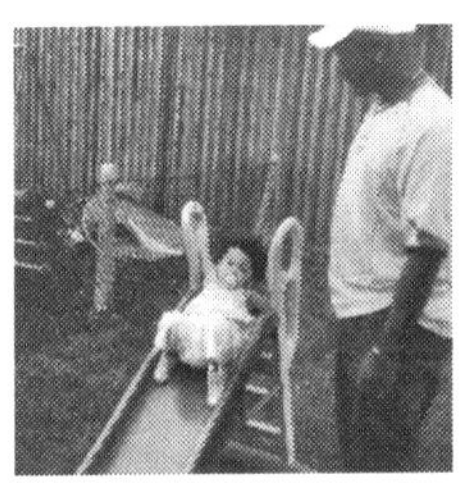

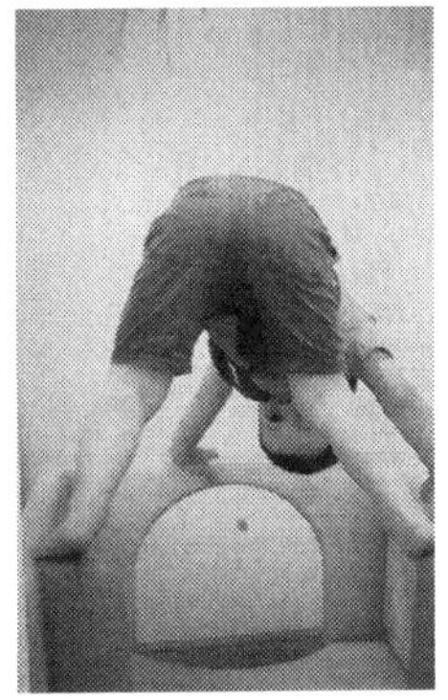
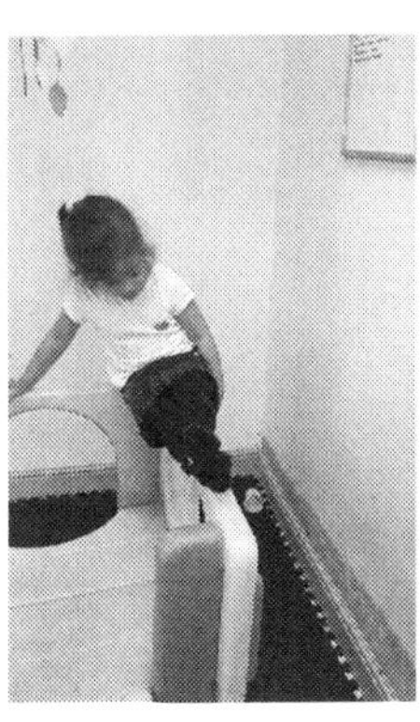

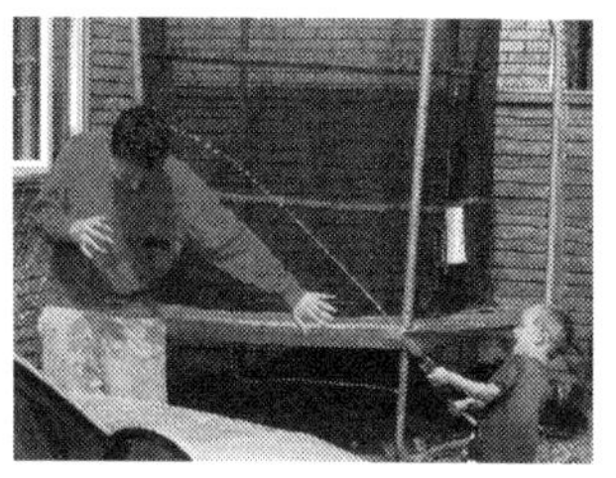

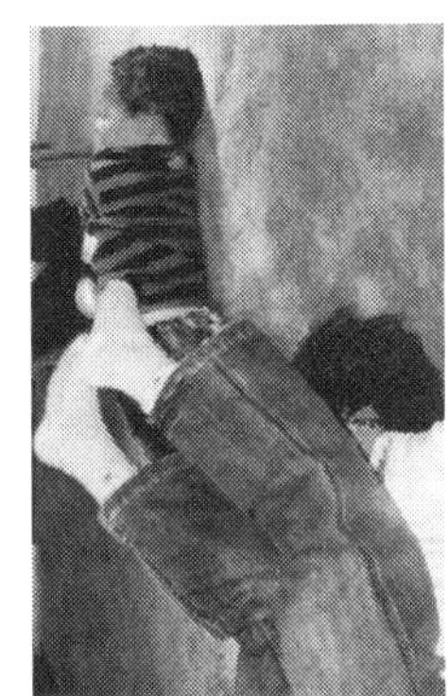

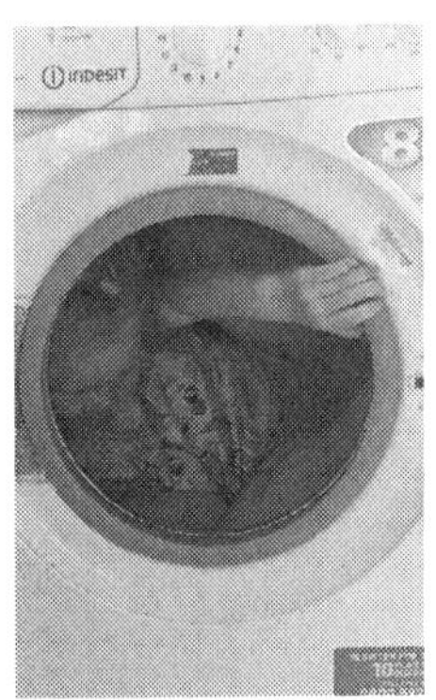
INDESIT

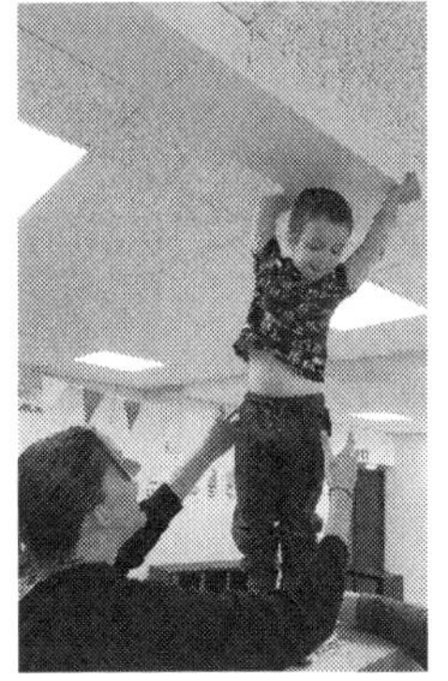

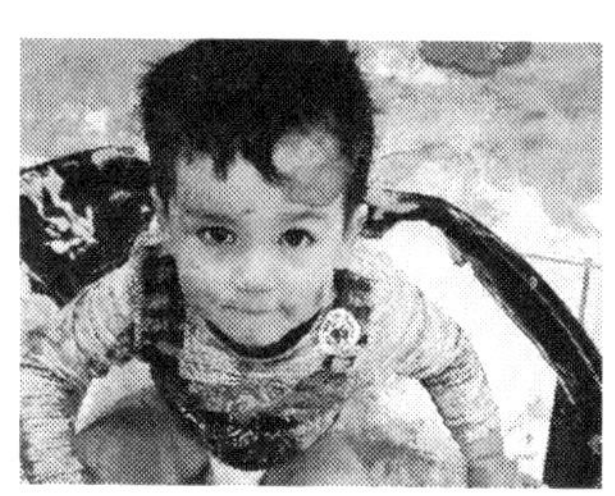

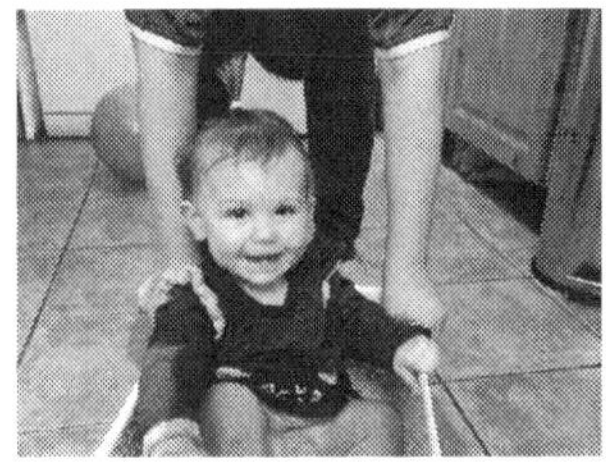

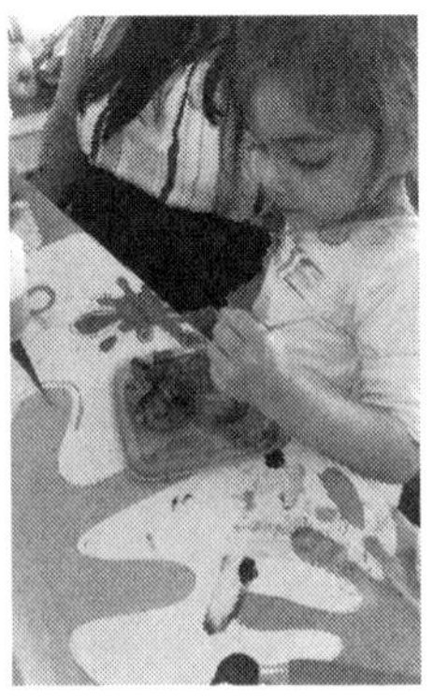

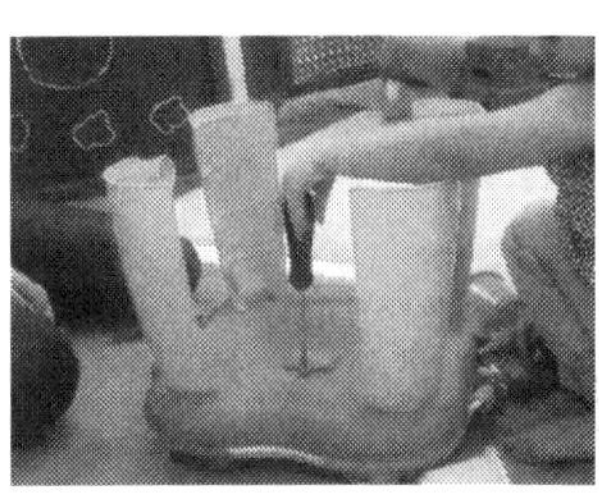

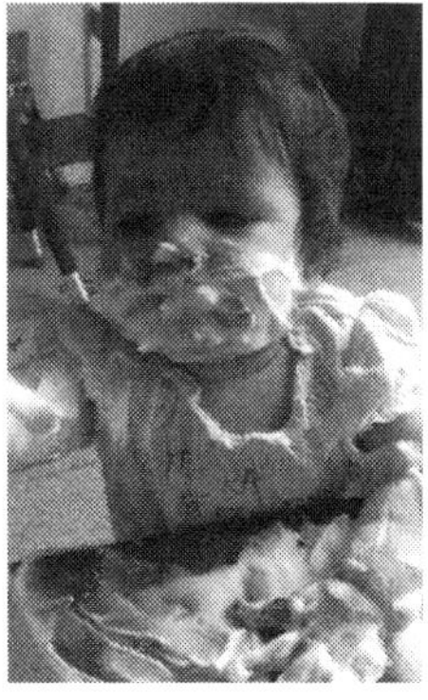

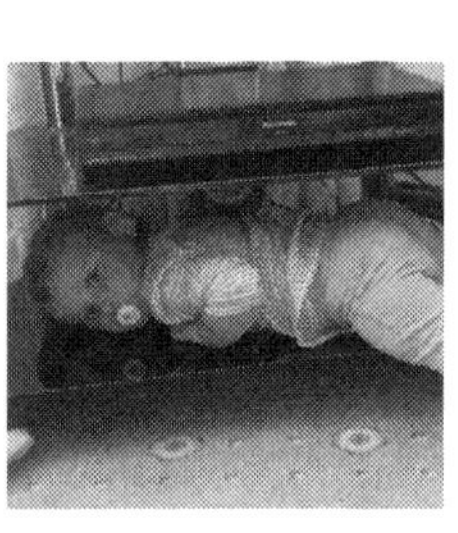

more confident in their ability and display much more confidence within the setting they attend, the number of useful observations taken using a Playwork approach increase substantially, and the knowledge of the child becomes key as they become excited and enthused within their surroundings.

The Playwork approach does not require anything other than practitioners that are resourceful and observant to the children during their day, to not interrupt play and to just *'see what happens'* when children can go with their own feelings. It does, however, need relaxed staff that can tolerate an element of not knowing what their day will entail with an ability to not interfere, unless there is an explicit danger to the child. Children thrive on consistency and spontaneity - giving children opportunities for themselves rather than implemented play processes can also be described as *'compound flexibility' (Brown, 2010 p3-55).* Giving children the ability between a flexible yet adaptable environment without adult interference, further enabling the child to play and learn independently, developing confidence and resilience away from anyone else; children do not always want to be around people or asked why they are on their own. However, children that do want to play on their own are respected but kept a closer eye on to ensure they are okay. The practitioner's knowledge of the child, usually establishes if there is some reason if the child is alone if this isn't a common action for the child; there could be a number of reasons other than play related solo play.

Dancing and noises
by Staff member - added 27 Sept 2019 11:26 AM
Children: 16 months

Notes
Declan can hear the radio playing music and he makes his way over towards the radio whilst bopping up and down. When I start recording, Declan is distracted by me and falls down but hears the pan he is carrying hit the floor. He bangs it again. He then bangs it on the carpet and listens to the noise. He continues to experiment

with the noises the pan makes on different objects.

Early Years Foundation Stage

Listening and attention

8-20 Emerging

Moving and Handling

8-20 No Refinement

The world

8-20 Emerging

Exploring and using media and materials

8-20 No Refinement

- Has a strong exploratory impulse.
- Concentratesintentlyonanobjectoractivityofownchoosing for short periods.
- Pays attention to dominant stimulus - easily distracted by noises or other people talking.
- When sitting, can lean forward to pick up small toys.
- Takes first few steps independently.
- Passes toys from one hand to the other.
- Holds an object in each hand and brings them together in the middle, e.g. holds two blocks and bangs them together.
- Becomes absorbed in combining objects, e.g. banging two objects or placing objects into containers.
- Explores and experiments with a range of media through sensory exploration, and using whole body.
- Move their whole bodies to sounds they enjoy, such as music or a regular beat.

This observation shows a toddler, who could hear the radio playing. He wanders down the room to go and dance, taking a small saucepan with him. When he trips and hits the pan on the floor, he is then distracted by the noise the pan makes on the tiled floor, which then develops into him experimenting with the pan and different objects. This activity covered 10 areas within the *Early Years Foundation Stage (DfE, 2017)*, however, as a Play practitioner; there is a different element of learning taking place. The child was driven by their own play drive, and ludic ecology *(Else and Sturrock, 2003)*. The child's cue to play was derived from the sound of the pan hitting the floor, this was the beginning of a play cycle *(Wilson, 1998, p16)*, this then started a cycle of the child finding new things to bang to attain the play back, *"play cue" (Else and Sturrock, 2003)*. This cycle continued and developed within the *"metaludic space" (Else and Sturrock, 2003)* until he had finished finding new sounds, meaning the game/cycle had come to its natural end. This was caused by two things; primarily, the practitioner interrupting his scheme of play and secondly, the fall. The practitioner was quick to amend their behaviours due to being caught with the camera. This approach enabled the child to explore and follow his own drive, continuing his own play for as long as he felt necessary; until his play cycle was complete.

Practitioners who want to do something, or are new to the setting, are encouraged to go and play. Children that see practitioners playing are more inclined to play and be playful. We must remember this is the children's space and we are observers within their space, not the other way around. We are fortunate that we get to spend time with the children, however a child's work is play and this should be respected as such. Children love seeing practitioners doing their own thing, it is also nice to see children ask questions and inspect what the practitioner is up to. The child is always happy to intervene and take over what you are doing or encourage you to try something else, this is the natural wonder of children. Practitioners who sit and aren't engaged in anything, can be unseen and therefore not taken notice of within the setting, working towards the child and their playful activity. Children will always approach the busiest people more than the ones sat still. I think this is something that continues into adulthood, the ones who are sat doing nothing can be seen as disengaged and *'boring'*, but those that are interesting always attract others.

Pre-planned activities

For activities such as Christmas or Mother's/Father's Day, activities are usually something done for the benefit of the parents - trinkets and things the parents can keep. However, it is key to ensure children are never forced to do these things, I know the parents like these things, but why work so hard to encourage a child to be independent to then suddenly demand that they take part? Using finger prints and foot prints are all well and good, but if a child isn't used to the sensation of paint on their extremities, then how can it be constructive to the child's well-being if they don't have a choice? The easiest way to inspire children to take part is to set up paint as you would following your own routines, but instead of getting the child, painting their feet and printing it on paper, allow the child to get involved without support, let them build up their own confidence to want to try, and then use that moment to encourage and show them what you want them to do by letting them see others achieve it. If you don't have children, then unfortunately, you will have to be the willing participant. My team always have spare clothes (those that love messy play, anyway), and if they don't, they are prepared to get messy, again - playful adults inspire playful children. Any activities you want to do should be created naturally through interest and playfulness, anything else and the child may not be confident or may lose confidence as they are forced to do something they have no idea about, even more importantly, each piece should be as unique as the child is. The process is far more important than the product, and a child who has a story to share is much better than one that has nothing to say because they had no idea what they are working to create.

Children that are offered activities in this way produce *"affordances,"* these are *"features within the environment that can offer play cues and purpose" (Gill, 2012).* The use of affordance is a key for the benefit of building well-being and self-esteem in children. Play cues, as a reminder, are part of the play cycle *(Else, 2009)*, and are imperative to Playwork Inspired learning.

Several years ago, I was working with a practitioner who believed adult directed and child-led afterwards was the best approach. I was working alongside her to show her my approach, and how it worked. She set up a painting activity, she was mindful about the colours she wanted the children to use and provided everything the children needed to develop their picture. She invited the children to come and join her after spending a long time developing the specific outcomes that she expected the children to achieve, according to the children's ages and stages of development. She told the children what she wanted them to do and encouraged them to do their work. After a few minutes, one of the children asked to use blue paint. He was discouraged to by the practitioner because she didn't believe blue belonged in a fire picture, we had a quick chat and decided we would show them a fire on YouTube and decide from there. The little boy, bored by this point, went over and got a big rocket toy and then he asked if he could watch one take off. I put the video on and all of the children then wanted to play rockets, they painted rockets and counted to five and down from five spontaneously. This then led to somehow making pulley systems to pull the rocket up into *'space'* and *'land'* on the moon. This then became what was too heavy for the pulleys and what was too light. The children then decided they wanted to make rockets and wanted cardboard to make one, which they did. The original outcomes that were planned, were achieved, but so were around 15 other areas which were completely guided by the children creating their own play from simply painting something that had been planned for them. This was the moment the practitioner realised the difference between child led and child driven play; the opportunities the children create and how the children do not need to be directed to develop anything as they have this ability themselves.

Unexpected outcomes

The above written statement about the way children learn once enabled to create their own play whilst using Playwork Inspired Learning, demonstrates children's capabilities to develop their own outcomes are limitless. As discussed, children do not need pre-produced outcomes, observations of children are often all that is necessary. Children that lead their own play are more inclined to take bigger risks, it is well known that children will only take risks if they feel they can manage. Imagine a child climbing a tree, if the child is used to climbing, it will climb as high as they feel comfortable doing, they may become stuck - as they didn't consider how they would get down at the time of climbing. Children that are used to being supported constantly may be hesitant at climbing without an adult holding on to them, whilst other children won't even consider anything but climbing until they have got as high as they can. This is a concept that children use all the time within the setting, children will climb and manoeuvre everything they can access, and frequently, the children get out planks and crates and use these to create obstacle courses. Young walkers ask for support and as they get more confident, they require no support at all. As enablers, we encourage the children to try first before we leap in to assist them, again, understanding our role as potential confidence crushers, it is better to offer the child to do it alone and build up their confidence, independence and stamina instead of leaping in at the first opportunity.

Another unexpected outcome is the language development and acquisition between children, the construction of sentences and the flow of discussions they have. Children that believe they are having private conversation will discuss without limit. Conversations can be nonsensical, rude and humorous as well as cheeky. Things we have heard frequently are discussions around poo - this is beneficial to children as part of dirty play. Children associate poo as being dirty, however it feeds their imagination as it can be seen as a taboo subject with adults within the setting. Children talk about things they see and have heard at home, such as making coffee for friends coming to visit their house and cooking and entertaining guests. The funniest conversations revolve around children playing home, when children are role playing *'mummy and daddy'* roles, whilst other children play *'the child'* role. We get an insight into their family relationships, dynamics, behaviours and what they believe the role of the parent is. Even the youngest of children who are at the babbling stage try and make conversation with the other children. A funny observation was witnessed just a couple of days ago when a young baby was doing a settling in session. He was happily playing and an older child walked over to him having a big discussion - the baby looked over at the practitioner as if to say *'please help!'*

Children with English as a second language benefit hugely with this; children who start the setting with no English are more inclined to practice their English with someone their own age rather than sitting with an adult. One boy enjoys sitting with me and encouraging me to read books with him, he quietly repeats the words back to me, and as he got more confidence in practicing his English with other children in his own time, he does not give me books to read, as he proudly tells me the words. Even more impressively, after seeing other children asking Alexa to play songs, he finally asked to play *'gummy bears'* a few weeks back. However, critically, the next 50 odd times we heard it, the song left our ears hurting but the little boy was so proud, we couldn't very well stop him in this new exciting development. The same little boy who came to us with no English, was shy and quiet, is now confident in shouting with his friends, talking to practitioners and plays within the setting as if he has always been speaking English.

Children often achieve the Developmental outcomes faster as they work at their own pace, developing uniquely to their own interests and ability around other children who are also focusing on their own play. This creates a fast pace, high energy setting where children's cognitive ability is constantly working on *'what's next'* instead of what is expected. A literature review *"A world without play" (Gleave and Cole-Hamilton, 2012),* recognise play as not only an important function of children's immediate health and well-being, but also for physical and mental health into adult life. It mentions the importance of the adult role being the providers of opportunities for children to play independently, rather than being adult dependent. Lester and Russell, recognise that these opportunities *"should not 'instrumentalise' play by perceiving it as a tool to achieve other benefits" (2008, Cited in Gleave and Cole Hamilton, p3),* which is what the setting works hard to preserve. Play is paramount to the future development and well-being of our children and future adults.

A perfect research piece that works in conjunction with this approach is based in Denmark. It is widely recognised that children need time for play with other children and that they are not pushed to learn and develop. Children are cared for holistically and are able to develop when they are ready *(Alexander,*

2015). Furthermore, when looking at the *World Happiness Report (2016)*, the countries that ranked highest in happiness scales are those that are leading in play based understanding, where children learning in a holistic and supportive environment is encouraged - in contrast to this, the United Kingdom is ranked in 25th place *(Helliwell et al, 2016).* Arguably, the United Kingdom is reasonably high on the scale, but research of early year's provider's shows that there is a lack of understanding of psychological development and play for children under the age of five, rather than target-based learning, such as the *EYFS (DfE, 2017)* which can lead to children to have lower levels of resilience and confidence into adulthood. Research conducted on measuring well-being discusses the requirement to apply more health care as support mechanisms to develop childhood well-being, rather than specifically recognising play as the foremost important structure to develop childhood well-being and development *(Statham and Chase, 2010 pp4-14).*

The language we use

We are well known in early years to be positive with children, we all avoid using the words *'naughty'* and *'bad'* and encourage words such as incredible, amazing and kind, remembering the benefit of positive language in how we speak with the children - further enhancing positive relationships with everyone. However, there are some things that we were brought up with and are natural when working with young children. When I was young, my mum used to say *'if you break both your legs, don't come running back to me,'* at the time I had no idea what she was talking about until a few years later (probably later than most people would have caught on to it, but that is just me). The way we talk to children when they are playing, even when it just spills from your mouth, could inhibit children's confidence. We have all probably said it at some point, as it's in our nature (and risk assessments), *'if you fall, you will hurt yourself'* - what if they didn't fall? What if they want to test themselves to see if they can do it? *'You aren't big enough'*- they may be not physically, but what if mentally they had prepared themselves to tackle the challenge on their own? *'Let me help you, otherwise you won't do it'*, the child wouldn't have tried if they didn't think they could. All of these things we say to children, slowly nip at their confidence, children wouldn't try if they thought the opportunity was beyond their reach. Could you imagine being told you couldn't succeed as an adult - we would feel terrible, even so far as to give up because you believed what someone else said to you. I am not saying I never said it when my children were little, because that would be a lie, however, once it was out of my mouth, it was usually followed with a quick retraction and a push of encouragement, despite me envisioning the ambulance turning up, explaining how I had failed to ensure my child was safe at the park. Children absorb everything we say from an incredibly young age, however these small snippets of doubt we put on our children can affect them for the rest of their lives. We know as adults we either push forward and carry on regardless to prove we can achieve or we succumb to others and regret not trying. Confident children will do it because they are driven to do it, children that aren't very confident will listen and rely on the adults' knowledge to guide them. So if the adult says they cannot or should not do it - then they won't, potentially missing a huge opportunity in developing confidence and resilience to keep trying to achieve what they want to do. We all know the saying *'if at first you don't succeed, try and try again,'* but if children are stopped at the first instance, they may not try again for fear of being told they can't, or just because they don't believe they can.

Playwork Inspired Learning is based on possibility, opportunity and play. I have had to write observations on many physical developments in the 22-36 month band for children who are 12-16 months, just because they have the ability to climb ladders, slides and climbing equipment, or balance on the middle section of the seesaw, when the reality was - not even I was sure they could until they did!

Just because dinky Doris doesn't look capable when toddling around a room - it doesn't mean she cannot shock you and scare you silly, stood on the climb on seesaw the preschool aged children use (don't panic, its all-risk assessed, and there is soft rubber matting around to break to fall, as well as a practitioner with lightning speed reaction closely stood by to help her if she does fall), however, she did not!

EYFS tracking

Children working cooperatively and alone produce incredible opportunities for tracking. By watching children play, so many things are said, done and achieved, it can be challenging to keep on track of observations of the children. As practitioners working in this environment, we work with tablets in hand taking snapshots as the whole day continues. Children are accustomed to this scene and no longer pay attenti*on to us* taking photos, in most cases, children's pictures are taken from behind, on the side, but rarely their faces. Children are really good at saying *'cheese'* when they see a camera pointed at them, thanks to the technology available where photos are so easily taken. When children are playing, it is hugely important to ensure the child is not distracted from what they are doing to have their photo taken. It is also important not to go back and stage a photo - at the time the child is doing whatever you want to record, they were so busy in their own play they may not recognise what they have achieved!

The main benefit of using this approach is the knowledge of the children, as we spend so much time watching and listening to small conversations and actions within the setting, we are aware of their emotional and cognitive needs within minutes of coming in. As they play, we know what the children are generally thinking, what they like and anything that has happened since we saw them last.

Just yesterday, I had an opportunity to witness the significance of watching children drive their own learning, the little boy impressed me so much as he is quite reserved when talking to adults. He came over and asked me what the little boy was doing in the toilet - the little boy was pointing at the pictures that children had drawn on the walls a number of years ago. I said, he is probably counting all of the pictures, but I don't know. He then asked if he could go and count them too. I said yes, and off he went to count them. He came out after a couple of minutes and said he got stuck going up to twenty, and could I help him. We then both went into the bathroom, and I pointed whilst he counted. Remarkably, he counted to twenty with relative ease, and he continued! He got really stuck at twenty-three, and with me counting along with him - he made it to forty! I was absolutely dumbfounded; he had always been so reluctant to count in any situation but felt confident enough to do it with me! I was overjoyed and he knew it. I asked him if he would like to tell the other grown-ups and he declined. He didn't want to discuss it with anyone and went back to playing with his friends. However, I had got to witness this spontaneous play led by him and so completely overjoyed, I have to admit being slightly upset he didn't want to acknowledge it, but I know the little boy too well. He would not have liked it, so I left it and wrote the observation up, with so much joy in my heart, it could have burst.

7

How does it work with the Early Years Foundation Stage?

Again, from the above statement, as we link straight into this section, I think you can start to see how the children's self-driven learning is creating their own pace of learning, which has some incredible opportunities as the child is ready as well. I cannot even say that he would have done it on my pre-school side, especially in the room with his friends, however the bathroom led to a completely unique ludic moment just by creating the right environment for when he felt the opportunity was available. To some it is just a bathroom, but to the little boy yesterday, it was his little counting kingdom - just because he saw another child doing something he wanted to try. The learning is available regardless of how it is presented, however, just by having it available, does not mean children will naturally use it. This child has attended since he was three years old and had never taken any notice of the pictures. This is the sort of relationship I believe all children should have with their practitioners, built on trust and understanding. More surprisingly, we generally work together only once a week, so unsurprisingly, I was genuinely touched he shared this moment with me.

In this chapter I will introduce more theoretical information as well as explain to you how we have achieved it within my current setting and the settings before becoming a nursery. I will also develop on the promises I gave you back in the beginning - which will further help you to visualise how Playwork Inspired Learning works. As a follow on from Chapter 6 - The Proof Is In The Pudding, the methodology demonstrates for you the differences between Playwork and the *EYFS (DfE, 2017).*

Before reading this chapter, it is important to remember, that as practitioners we only get to witness our perception of what the children are doing, drawing out the things we see children learning whilst they create their own beliefs and roles within the setting. We cannot assume we know why they are doing these types of play however we strive to facilitate it.

Learning is tracked by observations in this environment, which is why our role as observers become just as important as early years teachers.

When looking at the whole child in terms of development, the *Early Years Foundation Stage (DfE, 2017)* makes allowances for children to develop in some areas of emotional development, but it does not cover all of the areas the developing child needs to strive in not only their earliest years, but throughout their lives. In other countries, children are not in education until they are seven years old, therefore it is important to note, if the children can learn anything within our care, it should be what the child naturally wants to learn, rather than focusing on prime and specific areas of development that are started from birth, up until the child is five years old. Critically, the early year's foundation stage misses out many areas of children's development, such as focusing on children's toileting awareness rather than areas such as colour awareness and children with English as an additional language (who are fluent in their home language but not English). There is no standard when it comes to children and as we all understand, children develop completely uniquely, hitting different milestones when they are ready, not when we believe they are ready. Importantly, what isn't taken into consideration is we are living in a generation where children as young as three are being diagnosed with depression, anxiety and behavioural issues. It could be suggested that this could be due to these children having a significantly shorter amount of time for play and self-development, rather than having adults believing children have to be taught very early on for fear of being left behind when they reach school age.

The Early Years Foundation Stage (DfE, 2017), breaks down the framework into two sections, these are:

Prime areas - Personal, Social and Emotional development, Physical development and Communication and Language

Specific areas - Literacy, Mathematics, Understanding of the world and Expressive arts and design

Children who do not achieve the prime areas of learning will, according to the statutory framework, inherently struggle to develop the specific areas. To ensure the children stay on track, it is imperative children should be assessed at two years of age, then again before their transition to school - which then makes up the child's report for their reception year of school. Interconnected with the Prime and Specific areas are the *Characteristics of Effective Learning (DfE, 2012)*; these describe opportunities for practitioners to assess how the child learns i.e. Playing and exploring, active learning and creating and thinking critically. These characteristics, when used in conjunction with the prime and specific areas, enable the practitioner to understand and assist the child's path to development, interestingly, the prime areas are broken down into sub headings. I believe it is important to acknowledge these to assist and give you the tools to enhance these further.

Personal Social and Emotional development key points; Making relationships, Self-confidence and Self-awareness and Managing feelings and behaviour.

Physical development's key points; Moving and Handling and Health and Self-care

Communication and Language focuses on; Listening and Attention, Understanding and Speaking.

If you are an experienced early year's practitioner, you should be aware of all the areas above and rely on these to ensure the unique child is recognised, but also given flexibility to learn. However, to further embed the whole child ethos and recognise that there are far more factors the developing child needs to equip them for not only life in school, but throughout their whole life - there are areas that Playwork inspired learning includes. These do not need assessing, nor do they require another mound of paperwork to add to the pre-existing stacks required to ensure the child is meeting them. You can witness them through the way you observe the child and through practice and reflection. This recognition will establish how much this should be a part of the framework, essentially filling the gaps instead of focusing on small defined areas based on just one particular framework.

The Playwork Principles *(Playwork Principles Scrutiny Group, 2004)*, were developed for older children but should be recognised and worked into the *Early Years Foundation Stage (DfE, 2017)* as their principles are easily transferable. The following is a brief breakdown of some of their principles that should be used;

"1 - All children and young people need to play, the impulse is innate, biological, psychological and socially necessary which is fundamental to the

healthy development and well-being of individuals and communities.

5 - The role of the playworker is to support all children and young people in the creation of a space in which they can play.

6 - The playworker's response to children and young people is based on a sound and up to date knowledge of the play process and reflective practice.

Point 6 is what Playwork Inspired Learning serves to demonstrate to the wider community of early years, practice should be largely reflective practice. How is it possible that these principles serve children over the age of five, yet exclude children under this age group? Children do not suddenly wake up at five years of age ready to play - this is an aspect that children are born with, the drive and ability to play and create, develop and learn for themselves. Early years is missing this significant process for children. Critically, these principles do not exist in school either! I understand that children need school; however, children learn better when they have the right opportunities. The Playwork principles should underpin all processes within early years, in schools and throughout childrens' academic careers. Even when I went in for lectures on my course, Stuart Lester's interactive approach to learning was worth every minute of attendance as we played games, laughed, worked as a team and learned so many more skills that would not have been possible when sitting and listening to death by PowerPoint and taking notes. I use this approach when I speak at university too - it makes myself, the research and information relatable and people actively listen more when they are engaged; surely the same approach could work within every age group currently in education?

The following two are significant within Playwork and Playwork Inspired Learning, therefore I believe should be priority in the development of early years practice.

2 - Play is a process that is freely chosen, personally directed and intrinsically motivated, meaning children and young people determine and control the content and intent of their play.

3 - The prime focus and essence of Playwork is to support and facilitate the play process and this should inform the development of play policy, strategy, training and education. (Playwork Principles Scrutiny Group, 2004)

As previously discussed, play is being used for something other than how it should be used, this has also been agreed within the white paper developed by the

European Early Childhood Education Research Association, where it was stated "it is important to note playful learning or the use of play for learning, may be slightly different to play initiated and controlled by children as players, which fits with a constructivist approach to development and education" (Special Interest Group, 2017).

What it does not establish is just how different they are. The notion of play being used in different formats across the United Kingdom was researched in my dissertation and this seems to be the case in many settings. There is a difference, but this may be due to the push for children to play whilst learning through these techniques, and wanting to use play for play's sake, but practitioners do not have a thorough understanding or knowledge to push the notion of play. When you contrast this to the Playwork Principles *(Playwork Principles Scrutiny Group, 2004)*, I believe Playwork Inspired Learning could revolutionise the role of play for our children.

Primarily, with Playwork Inspired Learning, we are working with children's spiritual growth (well-being, resilience, self-confidence, emotional growth and the child as a whole), therefore we should focus on that to begin with. We have discussed in previous chapters that the children in our care need more than academic growth and these are key years for brain development - so whatever we give them now will last for the rest of their lives. If we give the children strict routine and structure, children may not be able to *'think outside the box'* when it comes to imagination; if we focus too much on the end product and helping children at every opportunity, we could end up with children that lack confidence in their ability. So how can we help them, and are there any pre-existing theories we can use to help?

The Leuven Scale *(cited in Lewis, 2011)*, was introduced to assess children's levels of well-being and involvement - the scales individually rank from *'extremely low'* to *'extremely high.'* The scale of well-being seeks to ensure the child's level of comfort within the setting, with extremely low being a very upset child that is clearly unhappy, to a child that is happy, confident and is self-assured. The scale for levels of involvement are the same, ranked from *'low activity'* to *'sustained intense activity'*, again representing a passive and low energy child through to intense activity using concentration, creativity and persistence. This scale is used by some settings, but not all, but it can be used as a good indicator to children's emotional engagement during the day. Critically, these scales can change vastly over the day, every movement of the child can change the level of their well-being i.e. the child that doesn't want to have their nappy changed or has been on holiday and therefore has been absent for a while. It is also apparent during the lockdown of 2020 that children may come back quite low on both scales due to having a significant amount of time off. We have been very fortunate that children have returned to us happy and excited to be back in setting - however, I imagine some settings may not have been quite so lucky. If the setting operates on a completely play orientated basis, children will consistently be operating from high to extremely high levels, this is due to children being able to achieve and persevere at everything available to them. This measure of interest within the setting ensures children are meeting their own levels of well-being. Children that have the ability to control and create their own learning may start at point number 3 while they look for what to do, but as they settle and find their own stimulus, the child will move up the scale of emotional well-being. However, a child that enters a setting where there isn't much choice but are highly motivated by practitioners, may in turn, be highly responsive, but it is important to develop the knowledge and understanding as to where these levels of well-being are coming from. Is it the practitioner's support that is enabling the child to reach high levels through their attachment to a specific practitioner and therefore the child isn't confident to try alone? Or, is the child reliant on another adult to reach high levels of well-being? These are the thought processes that are required by understanding, and holistic practitioners, especially when using Playwork inspired learning, ensure that the children are able to have whatever support is required from the beginning. As the child's confidence in their own ability grows, so will their need for support from the practitioner. I am not saying attachment is not important, as the opposite is true, these attachments are significant in the healthy growth of the child, however, there is a fine line between a healthy attachment and one where the child feels it cannot exist without the constant support of their key person.

Children that are completely new to setting can often be distressed, but again, as mindful practitioners, we recognise that children will need a little support. However, if a child is left to find their own areas with the support of their parent with minimal practitioner intervention, children do settle faster due to their own feeling of security and body language presented by the parent in attendance with the child.

Therefore, this scale is good as a guide, but can be unreliable when changes occur or when a child first settles into the setting after never attending childcare before. With this in mind, it should generally only be used with children who are established within the setting, are used to attending and are comfortable with the staff team.

Another interesting model which should be fundamental to any setting following a child led ethos, is the opportunity to develop the whole child, holistically, as you have discovered through previous chapters. *The Early Years Foundation Stage (DfE, 2107),* does not state the significance of the development of the child in terms of their spiritual development; preferring to specify language, physical and emotional development as the key areas to develop. The document, *Every Child Matters (EE, 2012)* however - despite discussing children's holistic and linguistic development - does not specify how to promote this. Babies and toddlers also need to develop further than this, they deserve more than this too, this has been widely accepted by early year's professionals, and as a sector, we are now enabling young children to have choice, develop their own play and adapt practice to reflect the child as unique. However, this could exponentially improve, by introducing; to following method; to practice.

The SPICE (Brown 2014) model, recognises children's unique ability and acknowledges all aspects of a child's development, looking at children's spiritual needs as well as personal development. This model incorporates:

Social - *Opportunities for the child to learn on their own and as a group*
Physical - *Using a kinaesthetic approach (i.e. learning by doing, through touch and interaction with the environment and with others)*
Intellectual - *Developing the capability to process their thoughts and to remember events*
Creative/cognitive - *Learning forms for self-expression, role play and fantasy*
Emotional - *Playing with others, peer pressure, feelings and moral reasoning*

By focusing on these areas, the prime and specific areas on early development are more tangible, especially in daily practice. The easiest way to achieve this is to work with the setting to facilitate these areas. As discussed, this is about looking at your setting from a different perspective and recognising psychological areas of development rather than learning areas for development. *Stuart Lester (Cited in King et al, 2018)* said *"when Playworkers modify the space, add materials and respond to play cues, they can explore what could be, imagine what could happen and what could become, just as children do when they play."* Stuart was an incredible lecturer, possibly the reason I believed in myself - he was playful, insightful, and truly brilliant. This is the key feature of the setting - imagination and creativity created and developed by the children and embraced by the adults. Another perfect example of this was created by the children through their new love of looking in the mirror and each other's hair. They spent a large amount of time attempting to brush one another's hair with whatever equipment they had (including real hairbrushes when one of them was available) and then asking to check themselves out in the mirror, which was higher than the children; therefore we had to keep picking them up to enable them to see what they looked like with their new styles. With the help of the children, we then created a hairdressers' station and the children spent time attending to their friends' hair, role playing what they had heard at the hairdressers at home and in any situation where hair was being focused on, and then attempting to plait, straighten and shave hair; just like they had seen in their own lives. This opportunity led to hearing many conversations around cooperation, receiving compliments and complaints, which also led to children both either taking turns, waiting patiently for their turn, or dealing with the fall out of a bad haircut (obviously, no real scissors were involved although they did have access to brushes, rollers, bands, clips and a hair-dryer). They extended this by using dress up clothes as aprons and blankets for towels, some children also used bricks and train tracks to create their own way to hold their hair like straighteners and clippers (they made a noise to emulate clippers anyway). *Gale (cited in King and Newstead, 2018, p117)*, further confirms this by calling this *"an enquiry into the yet not known"*, enabling children to learn for themselves, whilst ensuring they are safe. Again, by ensuring the children could role play without physically cutting hair or shaving their friend's hair (could you imagine!), in an uninterrupted form which was developed and created by themselves, because this was what their current interest was. The children experimented freely with their peers developing coping strategies when their friend inadvertently hurt them, tolerance when their needs weren't met and how they interacted and reacted with each other in these situations. No one knew how the children would behave or tolerate this activity, their level of understanding and the age of children this activity would attract, but overall, this became a positive and child owned activity for children from the age of fourteen months, all the way through to seven years old. No practitioners were invited into this play in the duration the children were engaged in it, therefore adults did not join in.

Using the SPICE model *(Brown, 2014),* you can see from the above activity, children had social opportunities during this play, physical play using a kinaesthetic approach, they role played from experience, therefore meeting intellectual and creative outcomes, and finally, as it was an activity that could cause discomfort and the necessity to share, developed their emotional skills too. These are all things you will have experienced on a regular basis, but now you are learning to understand the deeper psychology of it - I expect you have had the same lightbulb moment I had all those years ago! Children are regularly doing this, and have been doing far more right in front of us, without practitioners even recognising, and this is an incredible opportunity to grab hold and pay attention to what we have been missing. This slight transition in our mind and away from implementing any type of play, other than letting children play, is detracting from the opportunities genuine child driven play can offer. When using this together with the Developmental Matters *(EE, 2012),* there are many areas within the spectrum of ages groups that can be met by just using the above activity as a guide. Furthermore, when you use this in conjunction with the Leuven scale *(Cited in Lewis, 2011),* and *the SPICE model (Brown, 2014)* you can begin to understand just how significant Playwork Inspired Learning is.

From the last observation, you can judge for yourself, the opportunities using other models. The following is an observation based on a child who was 19 months old, but this time uses all three methods for developing their own awareness. As previously mentioned, you only need to be aware of two, but write the third for the benefit of child development (my setting uses Tapestry, therefore I have used that as a template:

Drawing
by Staff member - added 22 Aug 2019 12:54 PM
Children: 19 months

Notes
Olivia is interested in what the older children are doing and she sees them drawing. I give her a pencil and she looks over the pencil carefully and then draws some lines and smiles. She then bangs the pencil on the table and laughs. She continues to watch the older children and tries to write on their pictures.

Early Years Foundation Stage
Making Relationships
8-20 No Refinement
Self Confidence & Self Awareness
16-26 No Refinement
Managing feelings and behaviour
8-20 No Refinement
Understanding
8-20 No Refinement
Speaking
8-20 No Refinement

- Seeks to gain attention in a variety of ways, drawing others into social interaction.
- Builds relationships with special people.
- Interacts with others and explores new situations when supported by familiar person.

- Shows interest in the activities of others and responds differently to children and adults, e.g. may be more interested in watching children than adults or may pay more attention when children talk to them.
- Explores new toys and environments, but *'checks in'* regularly with familiar adult as and when needed.
- Uses familiar adult to share feelings such as excitement or pleasure, and for *'emotional refuelling'* when feeling tired, stressed or frustrated
- Beginning to understand *'yes', 'no'* and some boundaries
- Developing the ability to follow others' body language, including pointing and gesture.
- Enjoys babbling and increasingly experiments with using sounds and words to communicate for a range of purposes (e.g.teddy, more, no, bye-bye.)
- Uses pointing with eye gaze to make requests, and to share an interest.

Physical Development

Literacy

Understanding the world

Expressive Arts and Design

Moving and Handling

8-20 No Refinement

Reading

8-20 No Refinement

Writing

16-26 No Refinement

The world

8-20 No Refinement

Exploring and using media and materials

16-26 No Refinement

- Picks up small objects between thumb and fingers.
- Holds pen or crayon using a whole hand (palmar) grasp and makes random marks with different strokes.
- Handles books and printed material with interest.
- Closely observes what animals, people and vehicles do.
- Imitates and improvises actions they have observed, e.g. clapping or waving.
- Notices and is interested in the effects of making movements which leave marks.

The child was absorbed in watching older children drawing, she is then given a pencil so she could join in. She then draws on the table before banging the pencil. After this, the child then tried to draw on other children's pictures; again, this activity includes 10 developmental areas according to the *Early Years Foundation Stage (DfE, 2017).* By copying older children, the child is able to develop her own learning through observation of her peers, the child is having an opportunity to develop confidence in her own ability while learning coping mechanisms when drawing on other children's work; which the other children were not too happy with.

As you can see, the child had minimal interaction from the practitioner other than giving her a pencil. The practitioner then stood back and let the child continue with trying to copy the other children drawing. When using *the SPICE model (Brown, 2014)*, you can see the child social skills; learning on their own while being part of a group and understanding that she cannot draw on other children's work through her peers. She was participating in drawing, so learning through doing (physical), however, she also frustrated a couple of her friends, therefore accepts social awareness and thought for other people's feelings - and her own (intellectual, creative/cognitive and emotional).

The most significant part of the SPICE model being shown like this, show us these areas of psychological development cannot be taught to children, they can only learn this for themselves without adults leading them into it. These are the foundations to resilient, confident, compassionate children when they leave the setting, these are key functionalities that children will use for the rest of their adult lives. Therefore, these areas should not be overlooked and the children trusted to develop these areas without any interference.

Moving on from the children's holistic development from a theoretical standpoint, I feel we should perhaps move on to how the room has been developed for children in our care. This is where Playwork Inspired Learning comes into its own - there will be some new concepts and ideas being developed, based on Playwork theory, which will be more significant than the ideas currently developed on cognitive behaviours in children, according to any government policy within early years.

How to arrange the room to facilitate child formed and child led play is reworking how you envision the setting as a place for children to grow and strengthen their own ability, whilst ensuring it is a space for children to learn in dual forms. In the early years, there are specific areas that should be key within setting, and ours is loosely the same, however, we understand the dual purpose of these areas. We have social, cooperative spaces for play i.e. home corner, make-up/hairdressing station (child designed space), to enhance social gatherings, enhance group conversational language, peer conversation for working in a team, learning how to lead and follow body language, take turns, how to engage with other age groups that may have different levels of comprehension and work through conflict. There are also spaces where children can play with bricks, transport toys and puzzles so that children can participate in solitary play, enhancing imaginative play, resilience and perseverance when things don't go to plan i.e. their tower falls down, and their self-confidence improves when they successfully achieve what they wanted to. Not only does this work in cooperation with the *EYFS (DfE, 2017)*, it also uses our unique perspective to ensure children are able to build important foundations for play and personal development from a young age.

From this perspective it is clear to see that we are developing children's opportunities to learn in both an academic format, but it also ensures the child develops holistically - equipping children with the ability to question, cope and persevere. These skills not only help them transition throughout their journey into school, but it also gives them the coping ability into adulthood - which will lessen the mental impact that comes with changes out of our control i.e. changing jobs, moving house, friendships, relationships and generally everything that life throws at us. It is incredible what play can offer, if used without prejudice or purpose.

8

Resistance

Well done for reading this far - we have looked at similarities and differences, had an insight on how Playwork Inspired Learning works and how we can use it alongside all other theories being used at your current setting, or you can use it as a stand-alone approach in your setting.

When I put together my dissertation, I asked professional friends/colleagues, some parents and a couple of my team, who had experiences working within nurseries (other than my own), for their insight on how they felt my approach worked within the setting, and their overall thought on whether the approach would work within the wider community of practice. I asked if I could use their feedback from that and to include it here as I felt it was important to share real world opinions rather than just my own. Testimonials always work, as do recommendations, therefore, they belong and have their own place within this book.

Let's start with a really lovely piece of feedback I received from one of my parents. When I had started writing this book, I asked parents of both present and past, if they would like to add something to the book, to help me to help them understand the impact of what we do. This one brought a tear to my eye.

"I absolutely feel that the care Erin and Jacob received helped with their development. With both of them being summer babies I always worried about them starting school being so much younger than the others in their class, but when it came to it, they had so much confidence on their first days that I had no need to worry at all. People always comment on how confident they both are and they have the best imaginations - they always arrived and left with a smile on their face."

As I said right at the beginning, I have never been in a nursery (other than when my children went to school based nurseries many years ago), and as a parent, you don't really get the meat off the bones and see how they work from the inside. Other people have far more experience than I do in other settings, therefore they understand other theories, other ways of working and to be fair, a wider scope of knowledge than I do when it comes to what a nursery feels like. I have literally become a nursery; that runs like a big childminder; but it's how I believe children learn best. Outside opinions really do count!

Here is some valued feedback from my team, and before believing any changes are possible and explaining them, we should start on a couple of positives.

> *"Having worked in early years for nearly 26 years as a practitioner, I was always working in my previous settings using adult led activities, obtaining observations for children using this route. At the time, I wrongly believed that this was in the best interest of the children and the practitioner, and that children developed better following this adult led route. I know now that the above was actually not true, I started working with Chris, 6 years ago, and on starting, I realised the setting was mostly child led through Playwork, I did not initially see how this would work, but very quickly, I saw this type of learning was not only beneficial to the children, but also the practitioner. I was amazed at how many observations I was able to record... many more than adult led. Children are more relaxed in this environment, which helps them to develop naturally and definitely has long term benefits for both children and practitioners" (Harris, 2019)*

Over the last six years, this team member has seen this approach develop to where it is now, so is really obvious to just how different the approach has always been since she came to us, and to see how it has evolved over the time she has been with us. She has seen the theory become the approach it is today. Another, newer team member had this to say, having only been working with us for just over a year. Again, she came from having experience in other settings but has picked up our approach really fast, learning to relax and settle into a playful setting rather than one that was based on routines and structured activities and plans; "

Playwork Inspired Learning is a far better approach for children, they seem to be so much happier and confident in a child led setting. And as for us as practitioners, we have the ability to observe more great free play activities, as the children engage freely with each other when thinking of their own ideas of how to play or figure out a situation. When observing a child who plays freely, we are able to cover so much more of the EYFS, as the children confidently come up with their own thinking rather than it being structured activities to follow with a limited range of areas to cover. Personally, I think it also gives us a better view of their likes and dislikes too. One example of a structured activity turned into a child led activity; giving a child a cardboard box to colour in... when they are given the opportunity to choose their play, they let their imagination run wild and then turn it into a house/rocket/den, adding blankets and other materials to it - involving their friends, which also brings out their self-confidence, self-esteem and speech development" (Mayo, 2020)

These are just two examples of how Playwork Inspired Learning can work within any setting - even with years of experience within other settings, these practitioner's made the transition from one setting to mine, despite it being so different, yet have embraced this approach with ease, understanding and excitement.

I understand that changing the way you work can be incredibly hard, especially when it seems counter intuitive to what you have qualified in and learned to be the *'right'* way - Ofsted seem to want another, and parents yet another. This is where the use of space, becomes an amazing way to look at it. What we see, what children see, what visitors see and what parents see are different. As discussed, parents may see mess where we see creativity, and children see it as opportunity. Just like beauty is in the eye of the beholder

- the play space is the same. The setting has two functions, the production of a play space and yet, at the same time, a learning space. However, it is the fluidity between learning and playing that gives the setting the duality that children need to be able to play within the space, whilst learning for themselves.

When you go into your setting the next time, just sit back and observe the children. Watch their movements and how they coordinate themselves around the room, you can see empty spaces becoming playful spaces; reading spaces are re-awakened areas for large and small conversations. Just sit away a little and listen to the murmurings of the children and notice how they use their environment in ways you could never have anticipated. In setting today, we watched a preschool boy navigate the space all day with a seesaw - he moved the seesaw like a trolley, balancing cars on it and skilfully avoided all children that he could have easily knocked down on his little route of whatever he had going on in his mind. As a child with English as an additional language, he gently said excuse me and told children *"no"*, when they tried to clamber on to the seesaw. He was completely engrossed in what he was doing, and no one was going to stand in his way of his mission. Most surprisingly, he even managed to push the seesaw through a small gap without changing course or adapting his route, the seesaw glided straight through! There were no outcomes or expectations and none of the team stopped him, however, he had the best time today. He left us happy, confident and whatever he needed to play out today, I think he did that too! Some days, like this example, children just play because that's all they need - he did do a few other things but today was about spacial awareness, movement, and just having that time. I think we forget that children, like us adults - just need a day where we can just do our own thing. Sometimes I would rather just chill out and enjoy dancing to music or reading a book (that isn't academic). Down time is essential and whatever the little boy needed today, he did it with no complaints from the adults, no other children paid any attention and he fulfilled his own requirements for self-satisfaction. This was also true of another child who was playing in the playroom with a pushchair. I am sure you have also witnessed this in your own setting, but now you are beginning to see Playwork Inspired Learning being used, I hope that you can use this to develop your own ideas. I have purposely left the *EYFS (DfE, 2017)*, out of this, but if you wish, you can add them.

A toddler, who was playing independently within the playroom, was pushing the pushchair around the room but getting it stuck on toys and equipment already on the floor. Without any adults telling her how to fix the problem by tidying up or continuing to push the pushchair, she decides to pull the pushchair so she can adjust her movement, and essentially drag the pushchair more easily behind her and over the things in the way. Again, this is showing the toddlers independence, resilience and confidence in her own ability to move her way through the room, whilst still being able to keep her *'baby'* safe from falling from the toy pushchair.

The poor *'baby'* managed to stay upright in the pushchair and as infuriated as the little girl felt, she was totally committed to getting the pushchair through everything that was in her path.

The children in your care may go crazy for the first couple of days, they are used to structure and routine and you are relieving them of these rituals. They just aren't used to making their own rules, but will soon begin to regulate themselves and tell each other what is acceptable. In our setting, we still have set mealtimes, however, everything outside of this is a choice, we don't ask what these choices are, we just wait for their choices to become apparent. Some children will ask us to read books, others will go and build, climb on the climbing frame or play music on Alexa, barely starting one song before the next is already being shouted out. However, we are prepared, tablets in hand, and observation ready by placing ourselves across the room where we can see every angle and hear most of the conversations. Sometimes we even gather closer together and chat amongst ourselves in our triangle or square shape, so we can still see all of the children, yet they have no idea we can see them. This is our normal, and it works because the children think we aren't watching!

Why wouldn't you try it and see how it works? Just observe how the children interact when they think they are in charge - if there are rules in place, I can promise you, that you will hear them! If there are common sayings from practitioners, be prepared to hear them too! All of the things you have said and done - children will soon show you from their perspective and its quite eye opening!

Oh, and don't think you can't ask children for help either - children know exactly where everything is! A pack of wet wipes, knives and forks, cups, nappies, you name it and children are excited and happy to help if they know you will appreciate the support. The children with us often wash up, get their own drinks and help the younger children if they need assistance. We have even had our four and five-year olds taking walking babies to the bathroom and offering to change them for us too! (this offer has never been taken up!) Not only does this give children an opportunity to feel more grown up - it helps their confidence, sense of self and resilience as they work out how to do it, provides them opportunities to ask questions and even, say no if they want to. These elements are so beneficial to children and they don't just last a few minutes, these spiritual areas will last them for the rest of their lives whilst enhancing their *'feel good'* endorphins. Once a child has helped on one occasion, they will want to do it more. For this very reason - it makes them feel great - and if they don't want to do it - it has the same effect on their confidence, resilience, sense of self and also gives them the courage and strength in their opinion being counted, which helps them to believe in the power of their own voice.

What Playwork Inspired Learning does, is teach children the things that cannot be taught, cannot feature in developmental areas nor are being paid any specific detail to in early years. We need to ensure that we give the children the opportunity to develop spiritually in their own time with the right support and freedom from practitioners. We need to stop this and future generations from struggling with anxiety and build trust with the environment that they spend time in. This is the priority, once they trust the space, they will be able to relax and feel able to be themselves. Trust with adults is a slow process that takes time, and as such, we should not be throwing ourselves at the children to develop these relationships, they should be able to do this for themselves. They will naturally grow towards their favourite person, but this cannot be done if they do not know where they can go if they need to find a space away from both adults and children.

Exploring
By Staff Member 18 Sept 2019
Children: 13 months

Notes
Kevin was happy exploring the playroom today he was happy to move away from the staff

Early Years Foundation Stage
Making Relationships
8-20 Emerging
Moving and Handling
8-20 No Refinement

- Interacts with others and explores new situations when supported by familiar person.
- Crawls, bottom shuffles or rolls continuously to move around.

This is a short observation of a child who was still new to the setting and was beginning to find his own comfort within the surroundings using compound flexibility and independence to move freely around the room. Blank spaces promote spaces for nothingness, and interactions revolving around what the child wants to do. The child didn't want to be surrounded by adults and other children so he disappeared to go and play on his own. Compound flexibility *(Brown, 2010)* enables the child to play and learn independently, developing confidence and resilience away from anyone else. As previously discussed, everything a child does has learning attached, even if it is not within the *Early*

Years Foundation Stage (DfE, 2017) - it is still developing the awareness of his confidence in his own ability, which is fantastic for the child.

This is especially true in children over the age of two - how can parents teach stranger danger to their child but then to suddenly look around at a new setting only to be taken away from their parent at the first opportunity? If it were us, we would be terrified! We need to ensure that the child feels safe from the very first moment they walk into the setting, this often means building up confidence with the parents, which in turn, relaxes the parents and the child will feel this subconscious response from the parent. What is key, is the communication with the parent. Practitioners will often take no notice of the new child running around and playing - sometimes, not even saying hello (unless approached by the child). Don't worry though, this is not a shock to the potential parent, they are made fully aware when they walk into the setting. They are the parent and they know what their child should and should not do (they are the parent after all), and the first couple of visits - that's exactly what they're asked to do; tell the child if they believe they are doing something wrong, or stop them if they think they should. This pricks the child's interest in exploring and moving around the setting unnoticed, and the parent feels comfortable as we are not *'taking over'* their role as a parent. This is especially important for a parent, no one wants to feel their role has been taken over, and parents appreciate the fact we are letting them just be themselves. However, there is a really good opportunity as practitioners to see what the parent is like, the risks, the fear and how the parent is with the child, which in turn, helps us understand how we work with their child and the parents also. Setting up for a really good working relationship as professionals who look after the family (because that's what we do, isn't it - it has never been just the child we look after). This commitment from the very first moment of meeting the family instils our respect for them and doesn't detract from the care of the children already within the setting.

One really valid reason you may not want to use this approach in your setting is due to what we discussed right at the beginning in chapter 3 - why use this approach when it's no longer used in universities, early years or considered within any frameworks? Hopefully, by now you have recognised the overwhelming power that introducing Playwork Inspired Learning can achieve. Playwork cannot only exist for children over the age of five - under fives may not have the language skills required to tell adults what they are doing, but observations can help to fulfil every area of developmental outcomes for the children, whilst ensuring they build their own spirituality.

It seems bizarre that I am the first to do this, but if you don't trust yourself and your ability, new approaches will never come to life and children will miss out. Writing a book about prioritising play seems completely crazy to me, but I feel it is important and once you watch play, just being play - you will see the value of this too. Children don't need to do anything other than be themselves and learning this way is so crucial. I recently made a video to explain this approach, I made so many mistakes, said things I didn't actually want to say, and didn't say the things I really wanted to, but one thing stood out to me from this rambling post; it's all well and good knowing your colours, shapes and names - but if you are not brave enough to put your hand up and say, the children are already at a disadvantage. Playwork Inspired Learning prioritises spiritual development, to enable the child to stand up and *'be brave.'* I never anticipated saying this, yet, this is the reality of early years - why not give the child the full package? The power behind this fleeting statement IS the reason I need to share this, and the reason YOU need to try it.

I have seen practitioners learn to relax and enjoy their roles, where they are calmer, energised and able to have fun with the children and around the children. It's easy to say *'it's impossible'* but the reality is that its right there, it has always been there! Given the right tools and mindset, anyone can do anything – it's taken me 13 years to do this, yet it will take you a matter of hours in contrast as I am giving you all of the foundations via this book. However, if you don't, you've not lost anything other than a few hours of your evening. I have done all of the hard work, practicing, studying and finally getting the push to write and introduce this to you, you just have to try it for yourself and see how it works for you. You literally have nothing to lose (except what you paid for this book!)

Another reason you might feel resistance, is the fact that I've not really discussed how to use this with babies. Babies are, for the most part, tiny and immobile little things when they start with us, therefore they require a lot more care and attention than just leaving them to their own devices. Young and immobile babies need attention, there is no detracting from that, they also need time to learn to be okay on their own as this teaches resilience and cooperative interaction between other babies (we are talking minutes here). Again, it is important they have interaction with older children of other ages but they also need to build key relationships with their carer's. Their key person becomes the person they settle with and enjoy cuddles and interactions with; however, they do need to adapt to other practitioners in the setting so that when their abilities and requirements change, they are able to cope with this change. As the baby learns to sit and start to move, they do not need an adult by them all of the time. Their sense of well-being is developed through the nurturing support we offer them, then as they start to develop their own play drive, they are encouraged to go and explore. Babies are a tricky age for Playwork Inspired Learning, however, by giving them opportunities to be playful will enable them to use their own ideas, despite being very immature to it. Allow the babies to develop at their own pace and let them go through the motions of movement and coordination in their own time. At present, my setting does not use walkers (we have recently started using bouncers though, as a lot of parents do this at home). However, a child has a sequence of primary movements they need to establish before walking can even occur - therefore standing babies up all day long is not really appropriate. If you start to push a child, rather than letting them learn at their own pace, they may miss important steps to get to the point of walking. As discussed, children of any age will never attempt something they are not ready to do, so standing them upright to walk, before they have mastered sitting and pulling up seems a little wrong. Although, if they are doing this at home, then it's something you should do infrequently - thorough information from parents during settling in will give you this insight without having to see it written down.

Children's imaginations are at their best when they do not have anything to do, these are the richest moments to see what children can achieve when they set their mind to it. We do not need to fill children's time as this is something that children's brains can help fulfil, whilst giving them a sense of coping strategies, self-awareness and can really inspire a child to just be. Bored children are creative children.

If a child wants to throw things, give them the tools to enable them to make something to throw into, or if they're too young, help them to learn to think outside of the box and show them ways to achieve things. I personally do not like gun play as mentioned earlier, however, if a child has the imagination to build a gun, I will embrace this opportunity and help them to build targets (let's be honest, most children don't like to be *'shot'* if they are unaware that a child is shooting them). Being active and reactive is a large part of our role as providers, parents and guardians of children, letting play be play and assisting when something starts to become something more. This ensures that the children can continue their play without upsetting or impacting the children around them who may not want to be part of the child's cycle, however, when you enable the child to use their immediate play and add one small feature (to add safety from flying objects, or being shot), you are ensuring their own cycle continues with minimal impact on the original game at hand and the safety of those around them. Children do not need to be stopped, sometimes a small addition to ensure the safety of others is taken into account. Playwork Inspired Learning only stops or intervenes play when it becomes dangerous or may put others at risk - don't forget that the by product is learning. In contrast, this small addition may even actively open up more opportunities for learning to be witnessed, however, the child is just doing what they were doing before you added this extra element.

This is especially relevant for children around 18-28 months, they do not always understand that throwing isn't anything but play, but by giving them opportunities through example on how to extend play, and use it for their own purpose with a choice, children learn to recognise they can also add things to their play to enhance it further. More often than not, children will use what we add for minutes before moving on and making their own version of what we gave them - this enhances their creativity without physically impacting their game and gives them opportunities to develop new ideas and introduce narratives and bigger play opportunities. Children, as discussed by Miller, who stated *"the event is always open to multiple experiences and the setting is always in the process of becoming" (Cited in Lester and Russell, 2017).* This is what Playwork Inspired Learning is always - fluid and flexible to the children. The setting is never fixed to one learning process for each child, as the children are busy in their moment, yet at the same time, readily and confident on the *'what next'*, co-dependently or independently, working on the next cycle of play which again can change. Like the ripples on a stream, each ripple is created by one splash, yet the ripples flow outwards, slowly fading out before the next big splash or gentle ripple begins. This cycle is never ending and the splash is just like a child - you don't know how long their ripple will last, however, you know that the next splash is never far away, but their own play has a ripple effect that will either draw children in or be ignored. Our days are never the same and that is what brings more excitement to our day, children will be happy and children will be sad, however, there is one thing that is guaranteed - they will play.

Another one of my practitioners offered up another perspective - she works within the preschool that is attached to my baby and toddlers area (we split between 9am-3pm so that our pre-schoolers can play without feeling like they have to be mindful of the babies, and have access to more things to encourage fine motor and scissor skills without having our babies cutting themselves). I didn't add her quote before now, as like me, this is the only setting she has ever worked in, but she knows the benefit to the children with the age group she works with.

"Children that have the opportunity to choose are more engaged with what they want to learn and how they want to learn, if we try to implement a routine, they lose interest and become bored. One of the children played 'happy birthday' with another child, which engaged a few of the children, this then led on to birthday gifts, what they received, the ages of each other, age on their next birthdays, which led on to the age of their families and us practitioners. All of these conversations had EYFS moments attached to them and they achieved far more this way, rather than asking them questions based on pre-planned activities that were based on specific outcomes. Another activity, came from playful language - we were getting ready to go out and the children asked where we were going. I replied, stating I was going 'to the moon', the children

then took this idea once outside and played astronauts, how it felt to walk on the moon, and their view of Earth from the moon. This was all spontaneous activity the children developed, just because I said the 'moon,' rather than just saying 'outside.' The children in my care have opportunities to correct, adapt and work with their own needs and play ideas, and we ensure that we record as much as we can (sometimes there is too much), to ensure we record what the children are learning using their own play." (Collins, 2020).

9

Developing This Yourself

"Attempts to define the quality of play in relation to individual learning and outcomes are limited because the outcomes don't reflect the social nature of learning and the distinct qualities and characteristics of play" (Special Interest Group, 2017)

I do not understand why we need to define play or make it anything more than what it is, and throughout this book - I hope that you also understand that play is just play. Play just happens around us and we take learning opportunities from our observations of the play created by the children. The quality of play has nothing to do with learning and children do not even consider learning as a concept when playing.

As early years practitioners we really get annoyed when people assume our role is to just play, and yet, this book is promoting just play - however, you should now be able to say yes, we play - and thoroughly explain what play gives to children and what us adults can learn from it. Unless you can explain play, no one will ever understand just how vitally important and relevant it is in children's lives. It is just as important as water, food and fresh air- if we took any of these things away, we just wouldn't thrive as humans. Our childhood is what makes us adults and the good, the bad, and the ugly from our childhoods, defines how we cope as adults. For instance, I spent my childhood coping with a parent with mental health issues - it has taught me compassion, resilience and a strong sense of self, however, it has left me with a terrible *'never say no complex'* and a drive to ensure childhood is protected so every child can play. Young children are now being diagnosed with anxiety at three years old and Dr's have begun prescribing play to young children as they just aren't having these opportunities anymore. Perhaps this is due to more cramped living conditions, or the rise in flash cards, introducing children to phonics as young as two and working to ensure our children are leaps and bounds ahead of other children, whilst taking away play without conscious thought of it ever being really necessary? Children now don't know how to play alone anymore and are receiving tablets and using technology at such a young age and they are losing skills on how to make friends and develop key skills to help them for the rest of their lives.

Over the last ten years, technology has become more accessible and has become the foundation to children's learning, distractions when parents are busy and peace makers when parents are out. Furthermore, manufacturers are also tapping into this market by offering designed child safe tablet/phone holders suitable for pushchairs/high-chairs and even for when in the car. Screen time for children under the age of five has developed to the point where one in four children under the age of two, and more than one third of children aged three to five, have their own tablet *(Hymas, 2018).* Children are being steered away from opportunities of the outside world to favour the online world of videos, games and streaming for entertainment, therefore should it not be our priority to ensure children spend their time with us being children, being playful and learning in a way that is unobtrusive and natural to them?

Both the young age of mental illness diagnosis and play having to be in effect prescribed, are startling facts that should not be ignored. A study in America, described the concerns about the numbers of young children (as young as four and five) who are showing these symptoms, which then has the potential to become chronic depression in later life. However, by using dyadic play therapy, children and their parents are beginning to find and work together to try and resolve the issue *(Nauret, 2018).* Dyadic play is the process of working in a playful, accepting, curious and empathetic manner, just as we have created within the setting. Critically, we are not trained psychotherapists, yet we are able to have open conversations with both the child and the parents if they feel like they need support, and Playwork Inspired Learning gives the child open and unjudged opportunities to talk freely as they talk to us as co-habitants of the setting.

There has also been a study in the United Kingdom, by NHS England. They recognise the importance of play for children's holistic health and well-being, recognising play is key in healthy growth and development and a natural part of childhood. This study was completed based on children who are under medical care, however their research is valuable for every child - using both *'normal'* play and therapeutic play, and charting the significant importance for every child *(Tonkin, 2014).* I wish I had found this when writing my dissertation! I will add the link in the references at the back as it is incredible reading, further justifying why Playwork Inspired Learning is so significant (as if this book is not enough).

Children at the setting have no access to technology during their day, even after school age children - with this, children learn to cooperate, coordinate, discuss, argue and work together to make the most of their time with us. From this, we see dens created, Lego cities develop, friendships founded and disputes being rectified, babies chasing older children as they learn to work with children of other age groups and helpers in the kitchen during mealtimes. If they had a tablet, we would be lucky to get more than a grunt and the occasional moan that *'so and so, touched their tablet'* or *'they're annoying me.'* I sure know which one I prefer, and I only know too well, how important it is for the children to interact and play before going home to then watch tv or play on any tech they own. Technology requires limited imagination, no interaction (unless they use headphones and speak to their friends) and no core skills to manage life - whereas play can achieve all of this and more. Technology is taking over the world, and yes skills in technology are all well and good, however, nothing makes up for a lack of play either at home or in a childcare setting. School aged children are a nightmare when it comes to those infamous words *'I'm bored,'* which is why playing from a young age can ensure that they have imaginations and well-being in themselves, and sometimes just a little inspiration from us adults.

To be successful using this approach is easy, once you start recognising the deeper power than play holds, you will want to embrace it and indulge in it more. Watching children achieve on their own with limited support, in the full knowledge that they wouldn't try if they were not ready to, puts a new perspective on the whole setting.

These are ten steps to develop a setting that uses Playwork Inspired Learning.

1. Your setting is important

Recognise your setting as a space for play foremost and learning secondary;

you want children to be interested in exploring and engaging with their environment, developing their interest through opportunity and exploration. You need to develop places for social play and solo play and empty spaces for what may become, i.e. a new role play space, conversational space, or a chill out space for relaxation. All areas are already there, with the possible exception on a blank space. Learn to understand this is a space with many faces - what you see, the children see, professionals and parents see, are all different things. It may not appeal to all, but as long as you and the children are happy, that is really all that matters. The space can be explained to anyone else, but unless you understand it and its purpose, this is all that matters. Your setting is a unique space, every single thing the children in your setting, such as their play or their conversations; is a one-off snapshot that can never be recreated. Children's daily play will be different tomorrow with different feelings, different moods and different play. Just as adults have bad days and good days, children are the same; telling them to cheer up, never works - enable conversations, you are in their safe space - the difference is, you just happen to work within it. This space is the key to enabling children to unlock their potential, holistically, spiritually, and academically.

2. Children have the right to play for plays sake

The role of a setting that uses Playwork Inspired Learning, acknowledges that play starts from birth and its type changes as a child grows and matures. Babies from a young age can instigate playing *'boo,'* to knocking down blocks and structures, purposely for fun. As the child grows, this play then becomes more complex in its approach and its purpose. Being able to structure your setting to appeal and prepare for these different types of play is straightforward once you understand the complexities of play. Children of every age have the right to play regardless of age or background, but play is vitally important to children that live in poverty, at risk of harm and those who live in areas where parks are not accessible to them. Play is not a hobby or optional, it is what children need to do, and as childcare providers we should prioritise this. Wales is the only country that protects play and has a law protecting it! Therefore, as play is not recognised in England, play can be whatever we want it to be, which is a large part of why I wrote this book - Playwork Inspired

Learning is the perfect go between the two fields of early years and Playwork for the benefit of understanding the superior role play has. Critically, the role of play should not require a law, it should not be made legal, however, it does need recognition, just as much as frameworks and standards that we as practitioners must follow.

For children, the act of playing is enough to help to them achieve all of their own needs, although it is also clear that we need to follow early year's frameworks. To work with both the children's needs and our requirements, we need to ensure that the children play and we observe the learning, if you want to implement learning protocols then remember this should be separate to the children and their drive to play. We still do numbers, counting, mark making and all other aspects of our curriculum, however this is achieved by the practitioners singing spontaneously or sitting in a group before going off to play. The children have moments of learning, activities set up for the children to find, and on some occasions, the equipment we leave out for the children to use, such as our wooden walls and various sheets and blankets, but these pre-empted activities do not take up more than ten minute slots of the children's time and definitely less than half an hour of the child's entire day. This is done playfully but is not play (as adults we can make it playful, but the children haven't created it, so therefore, it is our definition of play).

3. Play is play and learning is learning - learning is a by-product of children's play

Children learn from engaging with other children, working together and working individually. They learn from children older than themselves and children younger than they are, as adults we can only assume our own roles on play and what is play, but it is unlike any play the children could create. That's where there should be a divide, adult's interpretation of play and children's intentions for play are vastly different. We can provide playful opportunities but they will never be play spaces until the children make it their own, using their own ludics *(Else and Sturrock 2003)* to develop, create and transform an adult interpretation to their reality of play. As discussed in point one (your setting), everything you see is a one off, a unique moment in time that will never be recreated, the play will never be the same and outcomes that you may observe, may not be there the second time around, each opportunity for the children will create different responses for each of the children on different days - again, this is the mystery of play in all its glorious form. You will work harder, yet more fluidly as the children move around and develop their own play, sitting in prominent places within eye sight and hearing distance will make the difference to everyone. We love the *"shh, listen"* moments as the conversations can be insightful and hilarious as they build up their own vocabulary and interactions with others. It's similar to children that come and tell on others, we always ask the child if they have told their friend what it is they didn't want or didn't like, and encourage them to use their voice to tell the other person what it was that upset them. This teaches the child confidence in their own voice and making themselves clear, it also establishes the other child's position because they do not expect another child to tell them. These peer relationships lay the foundations for children recognising their own limits, their self-esteem and enable them to develop where their boundaries are. If an adult intervened at the first instance, the children rely on adults to establish boundaries and limits for the children rather than with the children, enabling a child to develop their own limits, giving them the courage and confidence to be independent, but it also shows them asking for help, which is absolutely fine too. Using this approach inspires children to be free to have help whenever they need it but to be independent when they want to be as well - there is no wrong way for them to work and the children form better relationships with the adults using this approach. The relationship is created through mutual trust that we are always there and will not interfere with what they are doing unless it becomes too great of a risk.

This approach is much like parenthood, we protect and encourage children and only jump in when it's not safe, which continues their care from home within the setting. We do still cuddle, play and absolutely adore the children in our care, but we give the children the opportunities to come to us. Furthermore, recognising and encouraging safer relationships based on children's trust and ability to pick any adult they need for comfort at that time. It is much more holistic and natural for children to choose and they should be able to do this with ease.

4. Playwork Inspired Learning does its own work

If you try this approach with trepidation and nervousness, the children will pick up on this - the approach is quite theoretical but is also very natural to the child. I have been told by a few people over the years it is quite a *'hippy approach,'* but isn't that what it should be? There is no need for structured care - they will have enough of this when they enter year one of school. Children under the age of five need to explore, experience and experiment. Let the psychological values of current and relevant Playwork theory, work alongside thirteen years of experience and years of studying, remove the drama and allow you and your team to flourish, enjoy and adjust to this new way of working. As previously discussed, there is no additional paperwork, you can use what you currently use, or develop your own bubble chart to track the children's movements, interests and use these to contrast groups of children in attendance on given days, in a reflective manner when you want to reflect back on changes made, changes intended or general trends in use of the room. Interestingly, it is a handy tool to see how the children work differently in the space according to the staffing, the amount of flexibility and adaptability provided to the children and to see how the staff facilitate the freedoms recognised by this approach.

5. Consistency

The key to this approach is consistency, if you make the changes, you cannot suddenly retract the freedoms they were given, as it causes disruption, confusion and distress to the children as they suddenly cannot do all the things that they wanted one day to the next - you move in as a team or choose the parts you like as a team, and stick to it. This ensures the children are unaffected and the practitioners do not have conflict with the children trying to re-establish boundaries, which in turn causes the whole team to feel defeated and feel as if the children are acting up, despite this not being the case. Just like we wouldn't want to be told we could have the day off, for it to be taken away the very next day, it just isn't good for the children's confidence and is just confusing for everyone.

We need to value the children and let them play, every time we change the rules or boundaries children become unsettled and it can be distressing for some. At the beginning I mentioned this approach is freeing, not feral - but you cannot give and take away to the detriment to the children and their own holistic needs being catered for. From giving the children the power, they learn to self-regulate themselves and each other and develop their own rules as they go along. It really is inspiring to watch three years olds telling babies to be careful or their friends of the same age to be more mindful of others. This is what we are empowering children to achieve! Children don't need us to tell them what to do, they have self-regulation and will never approach something they do not feel they could do, therefore, why can we not trust the children to do this without us stopping their internal drives to do things? Risky play has become common place therefore, it makes sense that children should be able to be able to take these risks. Early years settings have so many risk assessments and we strive to ensure the health and safety of all children, not including the well-being of all the children in our care - we should trust the children more but always be at hand for any support children need, foremost we need to encourage children and instil them with the self-confidence they need to strive. A child at play should be celebrated and enabled rather than constricted to what we believe play should be. Once you witness the pure joy of a child playing without attaching anything to it, you will recognise the huge difference in what adult created and child led play is - I promise you, you will be inspired yourself. We have risk assessments for a reason and we would only buy equipment we believe is safe for the children - why not encourage the children to use it and imagine and experience it in new ways you wouldn't consider it?

6. Messy play area

This space you have to be a little more cautious with, especially with children under the age of two. We used to leave everything out and accessible to the children all of the time, however we soon realised that children love this area more than anything else available to them - especially paint! However, after many attempts, we recognised, this should be a little more restrictive and measured rather than children going berserk with every paint, every pencil and scissors (we never had children with haircuts though, luckily). Messy play should be balanced, we have arts and crafts, glue sticks, pencils and paper available all of the time without restrictions, but the paint is available to a couple of times during the week and added without the children realising until they are drawn to the area, this also applies to scissors. If the children ask to have these out, we do provide the children with them, however it is not practical to have it available all of the time, especially with children driving their own play. A practitioner is always close by to stop a child painting other children that do not want to be painted, or to ensure they do not paint every surface within the setting - also the risk of falling or slipping in paint is a real risk so we are more inclined to avoid this happening.

The parents absolutely loved these kind of activities as they were created by the child and led by the child - until the paint had practically dried!

7. Children need play more than focus

Children need play, it is a natural way for them to develop, learn and practice things that support them into adulthood. Children also need to fall, bump and make mistakes as this is foremost the best way for them to learn - how can they not understand that they will fall over unless they try? We are so focused on being incredibly close to children and protecting them from harm, that we are indirectly restricting them from testing and working things out. Children need to develop their sense of direction, stamina, strength and body positioning to adapt to new situations and environments. It also enhances their confidence in learning to cope with new and ever-changing circumstances. When children are doing the planned activities with visible outcomes, children strive to work to those expectations, which can have the opposite effect, where the children then lose confidence as they cannot achieve what is expected of them. This is even more apparent when children start school and have to learn written words - their life will become a series of expected results, therefore why not try new approaches to help them build their confidence ready for their next stage of learning? We are consistently told each child is unique; this approach ensures each child can work uniquely according to their own needs and desires.

8. Mindset of the team and observations

The team will also find a more cooperative way to work, the adjustment from working with specific groups of *'key children'* becomes based on observing a group of children that are playing in the same space - this enables more flexibility in their work and more spontaneous working. It also allows for practitioners to sit and do paperwork whilst keeping an eye on the children, which in turn allows for an opportunity to listen to the things children are saying and doing. As discussed in chapter 6, if the practitioner wants something to do, or wants a particular planned observation taking - encourage the practitioner to play. Children will soon pay attention to what the adult is doing. Using a child's own sense of intrigue, allows for a careful blend of freedom and flexibility within the environment.

Not only does this style of working, work for the child, it also works for the comfort of the team, as they're more relaxed while having the ability to be significantly more productive in taking observations. However, observations become more thorough too. When a practitioner takes an observation, try not to assume what the child is doing, if you see something and presume, then it becomes your interpretation of what they are doing - therefore, you should only write what you can from what you can see. Sometimes children's play can be crystal clear, however it should be a priority to only state the facts.

9. There's no such thing as the perfect approach

There will always be practitioners or parents that do not like this way of working, it's an introduction to something that is brand new, is completely unrelated to education and based on something that has no definition. However, by reading this book, I hope to have introduced the significance of play and how it can be used without using it for learning or to learn something. This psychological approach will enhance opportunities for every person you meet, even beginning to recognise the things you do and yet have no realisation of! Even if you use a small portion of information provided, you are moving towards a more playful environment which can only enhance the playfulness for everyone within the setting. The more relaxed the adults are, the more relaxed children feel and this can only be beneficial for children and their own feelings within this environment (especially new children who are alien to the surroundings). As discussed in section 9, it's more work and takes more thought, but healthier and calmer

– although, it will become louder the first couple of weeks while children learn to develop self-regulation and group rules. This is where the incredible transformation becomes a reality and the observation from a child led setting becomes one of a play-driven setting. The differences are incredible…as long as you are patient!

Some settings approach work in small chunks, whilst others cope with a whole transformation. Most settings follow one or two theorists and others follow theory to the letter - it is about what works for you, your team and the children in your care. This is an approach that is completely flexible, free and adaptable to everything you already do.

10. Practice and learn

It is hard work learning to change your mindset, and a few team members have struggled to adjust to sitting and observing, rather than working with small groups to achieve outcomes. What has been found however, is that there is more time on the floor for paperwork, if children see this happening and want to join in - these create opportunities for children to write their own *'paperwork,'* children get to see adults do things and will want to mirror this too. Just like at home, children want to copy and are reactive to what the parents do, and this is the exact same thing, just with a few more children and a fantastic way to do things. Children also love hoovering, cleaning, dusting, washing up, getting their own drinks and being generally *'helpful'* at every opportunity. In the ludic environment you have created, there are so many opportunities for children to engage and explore everything without prejudice, your children will flourish and relish in every opportunity. Just be careful of the hoover nozzle - we had a child sucking his stomach up with the hoover. He had the best time and when we told the parents he may come up in random marks - his parents said he did the same thing at home! By adjusting your thoughts and watching your children at play, you begin to see the wonder, children will make mistakes, but this is how they learn. Telling them off and telling them what to do, does not solve any situation, however if you build a relationship which is based on give and take, and no shouting, the children will start to listen to you in a new way. They will really take notice, because your voice becomes that of calm and encouraging rather than orders and stopping their play. I mean, could you, as an adult, imagine getting to an important piece of paperwork or halfway through an amazing discussion to be interrupted and told to stop? No ifs, no buts, just do as you are told! Now imagine this on a regular basis - you would become trapped in a cycle of *'why should I bother,'* understandably becoming disruptive, agitated and feeling irked waiting for the next call to order. What we are doing is keeping children on their toes, and the thing is, this will stay with children. We must be mindful that these children, despite their age, may get frustrated or annoyed when they are told they have to stop. Play is the work of children, so why must we feel constant interruption or stopping their play is any different? We are not teaching them to settle, we are teaching them that, although the environment is flexible, it can all be stopped at the drop of a hat. This is both unsettling and completely unreasonable as an adult, so why should we feel there any exception to children?

10

As A Whole

The final part of the book is upon us, I want to finish up with a final position statement, asking you to join my cause to establish better play for children under the age of five - for the sake of the children in our care. Playwork Inspired Learning is natural to the child, yet full of many different fields of study, to help us better understand why children should be left alone to play. In Playwork, as we have discussed, is something for older children, however, as parents, we have all heard the things our children have gotten up to when out playing with their friends. They are with their peers building dens, rope swings, walking through streams and getting up to all sorts of things us parents probably would not encourage if we were with them (we are talking pre-drinking age here). Our childhoods were the same - I know if my mum had known that I had been climbing trees, playing tag in the dip (big natural area with high grass, lots of trees and a big muddy stream running through it), I would have been in for trouble, however I had such great fun learning all sorts of things with my friends! Children under the age of five, yes, they do need to be watched a little more closely, but this does not mean that we need to interfere and impose ourselves on what they want to do. We just need to develop an understanding of the deeper workings of their play, to ensure that the children are developing at their pace, whilst learning on their own terms.

As you can see, I am incredibly passionate about this approach and I believe this could create a transformation, for not only the children in our care, but the well-being of our staff teams, our parent relationships; and also the future generations could benefit from the effects of these changes.

We have looked at safeguarding and how our work can make it easier for children to speak out if they need to, and our relationships with the children are more natural, to facilitate them to thrive in the environments we give them to flourish.

Referring back to the beginning, Playwork is not academic, but used in this format, play becomes the key focus for children's development in their own right. The old adage, you can take a horse to water but you cannot make it drink, is the same in how you can give children all the things in the world to help them learn, but if they are not there yet, the same is true. Children are better off learning for themselves and letting us observe them, only joining in if we are invited. We have to become aware of the impact our own play on them can create and try to ensure that doesn't happen. We also have to remember our own play is not the same as a child's - we can be playful but we can never compare it to the incredible playfulness children are born with.

I have to acknowledge that pre-birth children are learning all of the time, the transitions and learning that take place inside of the womb, however, I did not discuss this within the book as we only work with children post birth. What a gift though, the gift of opportunity within the womb and all through early childhood to just absorb everything through touch, taste, scent and observation, but more than that - trial and error. To imagine being able to do that as an adult, the overwhelm would be a real fear - no wonder children have such crazy emotions during this time of huge growth, with so much to learn and only a few select years to learn it. Children deserve to do this in a fun way, for themselves, with play as the very heart of it all.

We deserve to give children as much opportunity as possible to develop in their own unique way, we know that children are unique and this has to be better embraced - learning styles, speech and movement; even in my 17 years of experiences, it's rare to see two children that have been alike. Playwork Inspired Learning ensures that children are enabled to stay unique and their outcomes are reached naturally with children at the forefront of their play. They need to run and explore with their whole bodies, they need to experiment, combine, and experience everything, whether we want them to or not. Children need to make noise; this is how they develop speech; interactions and language that proves their point or asks a question.

Why are we using outdated theories to encourage learning in children? We have seen so many shifts in how children should be left outside to sleep, playing with shells from the second world war. Even in our own childhood -

you remember those huge slides and even bigger ladders to climb to the top? Hot days would cause burns on our bottoms and on wet days you would fly down the slide! There was not enough space to fit an adult to hold the child steady as they climbed - the child either did, or did not climb up to go down! I know we have become a suing nation, but children are being restricted in so many activities and given tech to *'help'* them cope with our technological advance era. Let parents be the ones to let their children play with tech toys and let our role develop the old school ways. Children need socialisation skills, to feel confident and to develop their own well-being significantly more than sitting at a screen, to learn how to cope at school and beyond and we are the gatekeepers to this.

Let the children feel safe if they want to throw a tantrum without telling them it will be alright - to them at that moment, it is not! It's okay to be cross or frustrated and to have a good rant, as an adult, does being told *'it's okay'* or to *'calm down'* ever help us calm down? NO! It makes us even more frustrated! We all have bad moods, bad days, days where we are clumsy, tired, silly and days where we don't want to be social - children have exactly the same moods. Children however, cannot convey that mood using language as it just hasn't developed, this is not the child's fault, nor should the adult make it the case. Children have a childhood to learn and develop key skills that they will need for the rest of their lives, our role is to ensure they do it as freely and openly as possibly with opportunities to play until they are all played out. Children are able to learn without adults constantly telling them what to do. Children have to learn to come out of these moods and to be able to manage huge feelings, it is our job to ensure that when they do come out of whatever mood they have, they're still loved and it is okay.

If a child thinks an adult can do it better, then why should they try? We need to step back and let children learn for themselves, yes there will be mistakes, but have we ever done anything wrong and felt the overwhelm of being accountable? As adults we know the pressure of every mistake we make, but what if the children of our future can achieve something really incredible by making a small mistake and not feeling like their world was going to crumble - what an incredible opportunity we can give! We are helping our future Dr's, surgeons, MP's, builders: these children are our future, it is our privilege to be able to help them to build their own foundations to our society. Let them get on with their play and ensure we witness their own ways of thinking and learning - without interruption. We all need to make mistakes, we are human but imagine what it feels like to be constantly told no, or interrupted during your most intense work. Children need the freedom to make mistakes and know that they can learn from them; they do not know everything - but nor do adults.

If we don't understand the rules explicitly, how should we expect the children to fully understand what we expect from them? Children have the rest of their lives to be sat down and told what to do, to follow strict rules and routines - under the age of five children need to experience fun, smiles, laughter and pleasure.

Playwork Inspired Learning is completely unique to any other approach that is currently within the early years sector - using a field of study, based on play for older children, yet developing it and using play theory, and Playwork, to develop why children should be using play in a way that works for them. As practitioners we should be enabling play and using learning as a by-product of this play. Children need us to be there to support them, but they don't need us to be there to hold their hand throughout every stage of their play - we are not the players in their game unless we are openly invited to participate. As much as we want to play like the children, we have grown out of their bubble of dreams, imagination and have to rely on our own memories of play and use this as best as we can. Adults play is completely different to the play of children, but this does not mean you cannot be playful with other children, adults and equipment in the room.

Playing is play, learning is learning. The two have become merged for the use of adults and to promote the process of learning, while trying to ensure it remains playfully steered towards the children and their own choices for play - with a little adult guidance along the way. We need to let the children play! Playwork Inspired learning embraces the huge role of playworkers in early years. It seems incomprehensible that there are playworkers qualified in careful observation and understanding in children's play, being forgotten within a whole sector. Knowledge in play is vastly misunderstood, untaught in college, further education and higher education, yet learning involving play has become the foremost way all settings believe children should learn! Unless practitioners develop these skills for themselves, the future of Playwork will be forgotten, and play will become a standard term for every activity children do regardless of whether it is adult led, child led, or based on pre-prescribed themes children have to continue regardless of their interest or not.

Playwork Inspired Learning puts play at the forefront of children's ability and opportunity to learn for themselves and learning as a last point. Children play, and we observe play and learning taking place. If children are ready to learn and want to take part in learning to write their name, read, tell the time or even to help us more, then we embrace the opportunity and show them how, we don't make specific times to do things like this. The child asking means that right there and then, is the perfect opportunity, as the child is ready and willing to learn. Some children want to learn to use their zips at a really young age, again, we facilitate that, which in turn gives these children the opportunity to teach their friends and help them when they are struggling. It is a constant cycle of helping, facilitating, enabling and then letting the child pass their newly acquired skill on to someone else. This is what Playwork Inspired Learning does. It empowers children to be independent yet gives us practitioners opportunities to help the child with their next step when asked. As is common knowledge, children learn better when they are ready - not when paperwork, guidelines or anyone believes they are. Each child is unique, and their personal and holistic development should be respected in the same way. When using the Leuven scale (with settled children), the SPICE model, and the play cycle together, we can understand the main components of the way childhood should be embraced and flexible to children of all ages.

During the lockdown of 2020, practitioners wanted the children to have more play during the lockdown - the *Early Years Foundation Stage (DfE,2017)*, was put on hold and children had opportunities to just play, parents became core educators, and those settings that stayed open, could ensure that the children's well-being was a priority during this time. Children had the opportunity to play freely with their families and within their settings as there were no required outcomes put on children during this time. I received many photos for this book, from families of their children out during lockdown; the opportunities the children had from their parents working less, or being unable to work at all, had huge benefits to the children. There were also lovely photos appearing on different settings on various pages online; it was safer to be outside than inside, therefore children had rich opportunities to play. When children were slowly able to return to setting, the smaller numbers meant that children had the freedom to move around and just play without anything else attached to it. The result of this was the outcry for children to be able to play more. Practitioners are already aware of the benefit of play, but it feels right to introduce a better, more natural form of play, rather than a facilitative tool for learning.

Playwork Inspired Learning puts play right at the forefront of learning and I hope you believe this too. Play is, and should be, the only way children learn and by introducing Playwork, it is fresh, modern and should appeal to everyone working within the early years sector. Change is long overdue, and we must be looking at more than school readiness - let's look at life readiness. If not for the children's abilities within life to protect and enable them; then perhaps we could cut the current status of children's mental health and coping skills into adulthood, we all know that children have almost adult forms of brain development in their own sense of self, and social identity by the time they are five.

Early years must protect children in play, protect play and never define what play is.

Reference list

Anon (2009) Analysis: ***Play workers struggle to implement EYFS*** [Online] Available at; https://www.nurseryworld.co.uk/News/article/analysis-playworkers-struggle-to-implement-eyfs

Bennett. S. and Hellyn. L. (2019) ***The Curiosity Approach*** [Online] Available at: https://www.thecuriosityapproach.com/

Brown, F. (1989) ***Playwork; Theory and Practice.*** Open University Press, Berkshire, United Kingdom

Brown, F. (2010) ***Playwork.*** Open University Press. Berkshire, United Kingdom

Brown. F. (2014) ***Play and Playwork, 101 Stories of Children Playing.*** Open University Press, United Kingdom

Cocks. V. (2020) Early years professional [personal communication] Gloucestershire, United Kingdom

Collins. L. (2020) Preschool practitioner [personal communication] Gloucestershire, United Kingdom

Department for Education (2017). ***Statutory Framework For The Early Years Foundation Stage.*** [ebook] London: Department for Education. Available at: https://www.gov.uk/government/publications/early-years-foundation-stage-framework--2

Early Education. (2012). ***Developmental Matters In The Early Years Foundation Stage (EYFS).*** [ebook] London: Early Education. Available at: https://www.foundationyears.org.uk/files/2012/03/Development-Matters-FINAL-PRINT-AMENDED.pdf

Else, P and Sturrock, G (2003) ***The Play Cycle: An Introduction to Psycholudics.*** Common Threads, Eastleigh, United Kingdom.

Else, P (2009) ***The value of play.*** Continuum International Publishing Group, London, United Kingdom.

Else. P. (2014) ***Making Sense of Play: Supporting Children in Their***

Play. Open University Press, England

Ephgrave, A (2015) ***A Nursery Year in Action.*** David Fulton Publishers

Gill. T. (2012) ***When you walk or you ride or you sit or you climb, that's affordance.*** [Online] Available at: https://rethinkingchildhood.com/2012/01/30/affordance/#more-1291

Groos, K (1919) ***The Play of Man.*** Hardpress. Miami

Harris. K. (2019) Early years practitioner [personal communication] Gloucestershire, United Kingdom

Hymas. C. (2018) ***One in four children under the age of two has their own tablet, MP's report shows.*** [article] available at: https://www.telegraph.co.uk/news/2018/06/25/one-four-children-two-has-tablet-mps-report-shows/

King. P. Newstead. S. (2018) ***Researching Play from a Playwork Perspective***. Routledge, Oxon, United Kingdom

King. P. and Sturrock. G. (2020) ***The Play Cycle; Theory, Research and Application.*** Routledge, Oxon

Lester. S and Russell. W (2017) ***Play and Space workbook,*** University of Gloucestershire

Lewis. K. (2011) ***Farre Laevers emotional wellbeing and involvement scales*** [Online] Available at: (https://www.earlylearninghq.org.uk/earlylearninghq-blog/the-leuven-well-being-and-involvement-scales/

Mayo. C. (2019) Early years deputy manager [personal communication] Gloucestershire, United Kingdom

Nauret, R., 2020. ***Diagnosed With Depression At 3 Years Old?*** [Online] Psychcentral.com. Available at: <https://psychcentral.com/news/2011/06/03/diagnosed-with-depression-at-3-years-old/26667.html>

Nicholson, S (1971) ***The Theory of Loose Parts; an important principle for design methodology*** [Online] Available at: https://jil.lboro.ac.uk/ojs/index.php/SDEC/article/view/1204 Accessed 14/02/2019

Pipertone, J. (2019). ***Interpretation of Lefebvre's spacial triad in the context of experiential learning.*** [Online] Available at; https://www.researchgate.net/figure/Interpretation-of-Lefebvres-spatial-triad-in-the-context-of-experiential-learning_fig1_317202482

Playwork Principles Scrutiny Group (2014) ***Playwork Principles.*** [Online]

Available at, http://www.playengland.org.uk/playwork-2/playwork-principles/

Ryall, E. Russell, W. Maclean, M. (2013. Pp164-5) ***The Philosophy of Play.*** Routledge. Oxon, United Kingdom

Saracho. N. and Spodek. B. (1998) ***Multiple Perspectives on Play in Early Childhood Education.*** State University of New York

Simpson. J. (2008) ***"Ludic".*** Oxford English Dictionary. Clarendon Press.

Special Interest Group (2019) ***"Rethinking Play" – The Role of Play in Early Education and Care.*** [Online PDF] Available at: http://www.eecera.org/wp-content/uploads/2017/01/POSITION-PAPER-SIG-RETHINKING-PLAY.pdf

Statham. J. and Chase. E. (2010) ***Childhood Wellbeing; A brief overview.*** [briefing paper 1] Childhood wellbeing research centre. United Kingdom

Sturrock and Else (1998) ***The Playground as therapeutic space: 'The Colorado Paper'*** [Online] Available at https://ipaewni.files.wordpress.com/2016/05/colorado-paper.pdf

Tonkin, A. (2014) ***The Provision Of Play In Health Service Delivery.*** [online] England.nhs.uk. Available at: https://www.england.nhs.uk/6cs/wp-content/uploads/sites/25/2015/03/nahps-full-report.pdf

UNICEF (1989) ***The United Nations Convention on the Rights of the Child.*** Available at: https://www.unicef.org.uk/rights-respecting-schools/wp-content/uploads/sites/4/2017/01/Summary-of-the-UNCRC.pdf

Contact Page

I would like to thank you for taking the time to read my book, I really hope that you found it as inspiring as I hoped it would be. This book is just an introduction to my approach therefore I haven't gone into a huge amount of detail in everything that Playwork Inspired Learning can achieve. There is a second book being developed in the not too distant future to go into more detail of Playwork and how it can be used to develop a more playful and freeing environment for every child that enters your setting.

If you enjoyed the book, felt inspired or are encouraged to try it, please leave a review on the amazon page - I would be hugely grateful.

If you wish to learn more information on my approach, then you can also find me on

Facebook
https://www.facebook.com/eyfsplayworking/

Instagram:
https://instagram.com/playworkinspiredlearning

Or you can email me at **eyfsplayworking@gmail.com**

Printed in Great Britain
by Amazon